First Art
for
Toddlers and Twos

and Charley!

Create & Explore!

Love,

MaryAnn Kohl

2012

More books written by MaryAnn Kohl and published by Gryphon House

Art with Anything

The Big Messy Art Book

Making Make-Believe

Preschool Art

Preschool Art: Clay & Dough

Preschool Art: Collage & Paper

Preschool Art: Craft & Construction

Preschool Art: Drawing

Preschool Art: Painting

Cooking Art, with Jean Potter

Global Art, with Jean Potter

MathArts, with Cindy Gainer

Art books written by MaryAnn Kohl and Published by Bright Ring Publishing

Discovering Great Artists, with Kim Solga

Good Earth Art, with Cindy Gainer

Great American Artists for Kids, with Kim Solga

Mudworks

ScienceArts, with Jean Potter

Scribble Art

Storybook Art, with Jean Potter

A MaryAnn Kohl Book

First Art

for
Toddlers and Twos
Open-Ended Art Experiences

MaryAnn F. Kohl

with

Renee Ramsey
Dana Bowman

Illustrations by Kathy Dobbs

SILVER SPRING, MD

Dedication

To Hannah and Megan, forever my favorite toddlers

~With wonderful memories still to come, Mom

Bulk Purchase

Gryphon House books are available for special premiums and sales promotions as well as for fund-raising use. Special editions or book excerpts also can be created to specifications. For details, contact the Director of Marketing at Gryphon House.

Disclaimer

Gryphon House, Inc. and MaryAnn F. Kohl, author, cannot be held responsible for damage, mishap, or injury incurred during the use of or because of activities in this book. Appropriate and reasonable caution and adult supervision of children involved in activities and corresponding to the age and capability of each child involved, is recommended at all times. Do not leave children unattended at any time. Observe safety and caution at all times.

Library of Congress Cataloging-in-Publication Data

Kohl, MaryAnn F.
 First art : art experiences for toddlers and twos / MaryAnn F. Kohl with Renee Ramsey and Dana Bowman ; illustrations: Katheryn Davis.
    p. cm.
 Includes indexes.
 ISBN 978-0-87659-399-8
1. Art--Study and teaching (Preschool)--Activity programs. I. Ramsey, Renee. II. Bowman, Dana. III. Title.
 LB1140.5.A7K63 2012
 372.5'044--dc23

                          2011028547

Acknowledgments

Special thanks and recognition to two special educators,
Renee Ramsey and Dana Bowman
~ From MaryAnn Kohl

In the case of writing a book about art for toddlers, three minds are definitely better than one!

Dana Bowman was first introduced to MaryAnn's philosophy of art when reading her book *Preschool Art*. Dana was pleased to find an author who felt the process of art for young children was more important than the finished product.

When Dana signed up her twin toddlers for a popular community art class for toddlers, she met toddler teacher Renee Ramsey. Renee had this same philosophy about children and art. Renee and Dana began to talk about how much a book about art for toddlers was needed. They approached MaryAnn Kohl about collaborating on just such a book, and so began a great three-way writing friendship with *First Art* as the outcome. MaryAnn says, "The team of Dana and Renee added a depth of experience and wisdom to this book. I have learned so much from both of them and I cannot thank them enough"

Renee Ramsey has taught process-oriented art to toddlers and preschoolers for more than 20 years. Her popular toddler art program, "My First Art Class," is presented in recreation centers in 10 different cities in the San Francisco bay area. An accomplished ceramics artist, Renee lives with her husband, Steve, and their daughter, Ginger, in San Jose, California.

Dana and her husband, Mike, live in Palo Alto with their three children: twin daughters Heather and Elizabeth, and younger sister Karen. The three sisters spend rainy days creating art indoors, and sunny days creating even messier art outdoors.

Thanks, Everyone!

Many educators and parents have contributed their favorite toddler art ideas and experiences to this book—our thanks to everyone. Their contributions show their clear dedication to young children.

Laura Hall Eisenberg, Brownfield, TX
Jane Chastain, Pickens, SC
Jane Harris, Roselle, IL
Angela Hendrickson, Coon Rapids, MN
Jeanie Herrod, Columbia, SC
Ardis Kosmala, Clinton Township, MI
Jayna Ledbetter, Greenville, Sc
Elaine Magud, Manteca, CA
Heidi Maier, Ocala, FL
Tracey Neumarke, Chicago, IL
Julie Peck, Jacksonville, FL
Pat Ritter, Lexington park, MD
Ellyn Schaffner, Halkirk, Alberta, Canana
Lee Schauer, Milwaukee, WI
Zanni Van Antwerp, Henderson, NV
Kreshna Warnock, Long Beach, CA
Cynthia Wilmarth, Mauna Lani, Hawaii

Table of Contents

Introduction

Who Are Toddlers and Twos?

Toddlers and twos are unique. They are separating from mommy and daddy and beginning to become independent people with their own preferences. Their outright declarations of "By myself!" or "No, no, no!" can be challenging. Because toddlers and twos are going through many changes of independence and separation, they often are uncertain or resistant during this time. Support and encouragement are key to making this transition time a happy one. A toddler or two-year-old may resist an activity one day and then welcome the very same activity the next day. Toddlers and twos offer adults a unique challenge to be flexible and patient, along with the joy of helping them grow through exploration and discovery.

Toddlers and Twos:
- Seek new and interesting stimuli
- Are often fearful of strangers, but are able to adjust
- Are perfecting fine motor skills
- Are usually somewhat anxious about separation from parents
- Like predictable routines, but are able to adjust
- Have a sense of "mine" and are learning "not mine"
- Are willing to experiment with art materials

Every toddler and two-year-old has a unique personality as well as a unique level and pace of development. Like snowflakes, no two children are alike or achieve the same skill level at the same time or in the same exact way. Temperament and development must be taken into account when planning and preparing art experiences.

Temperament varies widely: Some toddlers and twos are sensitive, while others seem resistant to distress. Some throw tantrums, while others are flexible. And of course, most toddlers and twos are somewhere in between. Feisty, fearful, adaptable, shy, docile, cautious, positive, negative, moody, intense, distracted, and active are all traits that apply to one child or another—sometimes to the same child all in the same day! Let your special child's temperament help you predict which art activities will work best on any given day. If it does not work today, try it tomorrow! The key to working with toddlers and twos is to be flexible, supportive, and nurturing. So, take a deep breath, and jump in!

The following "Toddler's Creed" appeared in the syndicated weekly newspaper column Families Today by T. Berry Brazelton and is a humorous reminder of normal behavior.

"Toddler's Creed"

If I want it, it's mine.

If I give it to you and change my mind later, it's mine.

If I can take it away from you, it's mine.

If I had it a little while ago, it's mine.

If it's mine, it will never belong to anybody else, no matter what.

If we are building something together, all the pieces are mine.

If it looks just like mine, it is mine.

—Reprinted with permission from T. Berry Brazelton

It's the Process, Not the Product

Toddlers and twos explore art as a learning experience or an experiment, discovering what is stimulating and interesting. They are more interested in *doing* art rather than making a finished product. During the process, toddlers and twos discover their own independence as well as the mystery of combinations, the joy of exploration, the delight of creating, and the frustration of challenges—all important pieces in the puzzle of learning. Whatever the resulting artwork—whether it is a bright, sticky glob or a gallery-worthy masterpiece—to a toddler or two-year-old, it is only the *result* of "doing art," not the *reason* for doing art.

To communicate to toddlers and twos that the process is indeed as important as they believe, use insightful, open-ended comments that will encourage each child to feel free to explore. The following are some examples:

- Tell me about your artwork (painting, drawing, playdough, and so on).
- Did you like doing this? Did you like making this?
- Show me the fluffy part.
- I see you've used many colors!
- How does the paint feel?
- Look at the bright yellow!
- What a big design!
- I see you've made your own shade of brown.

The art process allows toddlers and twos to explore, discover, and manipulate their worlds. Sometimes the process can be sensory, such as feeling slippery cool paint on bare fingers. Other times it is a mysterious surprise as colors blend unexpectedly or a blob of playdough takes form. Art process can be a way to "get the wiggles out" or to smash a ball of

clay instead of another child. The adult's job is simply to allow this process to happen! Provide interesting materials, and then sit back and watch closely (but unobtrusively). Offer help with unruly materials and cleanup, but do not make art samples to copy, as this will limit the possibilities of process and hinder the wonder of discovery.

Cynthia Willmarth, child care provider for young children, comments about the art explored in her childcare center. She says, "Two-year-olds do only open-ended process art in my class, as do the three-, four-, and five-year-olds. A few years ago, all the children, no matter what their ages, did art "projects" or crafts. But after thinking this over and reading up on child development, I decided to toss out all of the craftsy projects and fill our art centers with process art. We stock the art corner with all kinds of writing instruments, varieties of papers, glue, paste, tapes, paints, chalk, fabric, yarn, scissors, and natural materials (coconut fiber, coconuts, leaves, dried flowers), bins of collected collage materials, and recycled materials like cardboard tubes, plastic milk jugs, old envelopes and junk mail, and on and on. You should see all the creativity that comes from doing art this way! Art is so much more exciting than it used to be! Once in awhile we will have the children "make something" for Mother's Day or Father's Day, but still, they make it as they choose, in their own unique way. The process really is more important than the product when working with young children, and it's great being a teacher doing art this way."

How to Use This Book

First Art for Toddlers and Twos is organized into five chapters covering a variety of art explorations for children ages one through three, including:

- Paint activities
- Dough and clay activities
- Making marks in various ways
- Sticking on and gluing things
- Making prints

Within each chapter, the activities are presented progressively, starting with the easiest and most basic to those that build on basic skills. Each activity has a list of materials, adult preparation suggestions, and the art activity steps for toddlers and twos. Many activities include tips to "smooth out the bumps" and promote successful art experiences, and variations are included to enhance and expand each activity. (The activities often contain surprising adaptations!) In addition, you will find actual stories throughout the chapters of real children doing real art. Each activity has icons to assist you in choosing activities based on how much adult time is needed for preparation, as well as numerous other attributes (see page 12 for icon descriptions). Most important, this book is meant to be used and enjoyed every day, rain or shine, with young children (and anyone else who wants to join in the fun!). Activities can be repeated over and over, materials may be substituted, and the artwork can be saved or not.

Using the Icons

Each art activity has a list of icons that will help you select activities as well as make the activities more accessible and usable. Keep in mind that the icons are suggestions only, because no two children are ever alike. Use these icons as guides for selecting art activities, not as rules.

Adult Preparation/Planning

The *Adult Prep/Plan* icon indicates the degree of planning or preparation time you will need to collect materials, set up the art activity, and supervise it. Icons shown indicate planning that is easy, slightly involved, or most involved. Note that the *Prepare* section of each art activity is for adults to do, and the *Process* section is for the child to do.

Activity Level: Quiet or Active

Some art activities (and some toddlers and twos!) are naturally calm and quiet, while others are more active and noisy. The *Activity Level* icon alerts you to art experiences that are one or the other, although of course, individual children can change even a quiet activity to a noisy one in a matter of seconds!

First Art Cleanup

Toddlers and twos like to clean up often during art activities when their hands become covered in paint or get sticky. The *Soapy Sponge* icon indicates that you should provide either a bucket of soapy water with an old towel for independent hand washing or a fat, wet sponge for easy finger wiping.

Art Clothes

When toddlers and twos need to wear art clothes for messy projects, the *Art Clothes* icon appears. Children can wear a simple apron or smock or an old T-shirt over their clothes. Or, they can have an entire set of old play clothes to wear solely for art activities. Art clothes do not need to be washed very often, if at all. Simply let the art clothes dry and watch them develop a unique appearance!

Group

The *Group* icon appears when the activity works best with a group. Most activities lend themselves to both groups and individuals, so the icon appears only when a group is specifically recommended.

Outdoors

If an activity must be done outdoors, an *Outdoors* icon appears. Most activities can be enjoyed equally either indoors or out, so the icon is listed only when the activity *must* be done outdoors.

Caution

The *Caution* icon appears for activities using materials that may be sharp, hot, electrical, or include small objects. These activities require extra supervision and care. Safety should be a prime concern with children at all times. Never leave a toddler or two-year-old unattended. All activities require supervision of objects that children may put into their mouths, eyes, or ears. See page 14 for further discussion about safety.

Getting Ready!

Being prepared makes art more enjoyable for everyone involved. Here are some tips for working with toddlers and twos, and for their general well-being and comfort.

Covered Workspace

Cover the workspace with newspaper, whether it is a table, floor, chair, wall, or countertop. Tape the newspaper down to prevent wiggles and spills. It's much easier to bunch up sheets of paint-covered, sticky newspaper and find a clean space underneath than it is to clean up uncovered workspaces. Other recommended alternative workspace coverings are flat sheets of cardboard, old shower curtains, plastic or vinyl tablecloths, wide butcher paper, or roll ends of newsprint from a local newspaper print shop.

Handy Cleanup

Make cleanup with toddlers and twos easy and independent. Place a wet sponge; a wet, folded, old towel; or pads of damp paper towels next to the art project for toddlers and twos to wipe their fingers as needed. Rather than having children run to the sink, fill a bucket with warm soapy water, and place it near the workspace. Then add a few old towels for drying hands. A few damp rags and sponges are handy for wiping spills, tidying up, and cleaning splatters as necessary.

The Cover-Up

The most successful cover-ups for toddlers and twos are art clothes that are worn for art only. Toddlers and twos (and adults) can then enjoy art activities free of worries about clothing stains and spills. Art clothes might consist of a slip-on T-shirt, easy pull-on pants, and old Velcro-style sneakers, all of which are easy and quick to put on and take off. Art clothes become unique with time and are often a source of pride! An old apron, Dad's old shirt with the sleeves cut off, a smock, or a paint shirt are all helpful cover-ups, too. Another easy idea is to cut an old vinyl tablecloth into a smock shape that fits over a child's head and ties behind with strips of elastic sewn on the sides.

Tips

- Toddlers and twos usually work most comfortably either standing or kneeling. If they are sitting, their feet should touch the floor.
- Create a separate drying area covered with newspapers for wet projects to dry undisturbed. Carry drippy artwork flat on a sheet of newspaper to the drying area. Watch out for wind currents that may lift wet projects into the air!
- Consider protecting a larger circle of space (floors, walls, and carpets, and maybe even ceilings!) around the workspace from stray splatters.
- Most paints and dyes will stain skin, but after several baths or showers, the color will fade and eventually disappear.
- Shallow containers are often recommended for art materials. These include cookie sheets, flat baking pans, plastic trays, flat dishes, plates, and tofu containers.
- It's never too late to start collecting recyclables for art. Save collage materials, fabric and paper scraps, foam grocery trays, yarn, sewing trims, junk mail, sticks, and pebbles. See the collage list on pages XX–XX for more suggestions. Use heavy plastic storage bags, shoeboxes, or any other containers on hand for storage.
- Activities for toddlers and twos are generally indoor activities unless specifically noted as outdoor activities.
- Once is never enough for most toddlers and twos! Repeat activities over and over, and allow children to make one or many art projects. Have plenty of paper and supplies on hand for multiple art experiences. The more they explore and create, the more they learn.

All Important: Safety

- Safety with toddlers and twos should be of prime concern at all times.
- Never leave a toddler or two-year-old unattended.
- All art activities require attentive supervision and care.
- If working with smaller objects for collage or sorting, always sit one-on-one with the child to supervise closely.
- Be especially aware of objects that are small enough to be swallowed, and pointed objects that may poke. Also remember when using commercial art supplies to use only those that are labeled "nontoxic."
- Because toddlers and twos like to test objects with their lips and tongues, use a choke tube to assess which items are small enough to be a choking hazard. Small parts "testers" or choke tubes are available at hardware stores and better toy stores. To test if a toy or other object is potentially dangerous because of its size, place it—without compressing it—into the tube. If it fits entirely within the tube in any way, it should not be used by children under the age of three or any others who still put things into their mouths. Remember that children have choked on toys that pass the choke tube cylinder test. If a toddler or two-year-old tends to put things into her mouth, avoid objects that are smaller than her fist or that fit through a cardboard toilet paper roll. Small items that are particularly attractive to toddlers and twos (but are extremely risky) include balloons, pennies, marbles, staples, tacks, and paperclips. Watch for and heed the following warning on some toys and products: "Warning: CHOKING HAZARD: Small Parts. Not For Children Under 3."

Early Experiences with Process Art—The Place to Begin with Toddlers and Twos

Gather a number of large, wonderful materials that toddlers and two-year-olds can use independently (but supervised, of course). Place there within their reach and watch their creativity soar! The adult's delightfully easy job is to sit back and observe without giving directions, assistance, or their "expert" opinion!

Materials

containers
newspaper

A few art materials such as:

- chalk
- clear tape (weighted tape dispenser)
- collage materials on hand (see page 80–81)
- cotton balls
- crayons
- envelopes
- fabric scraps
- feathers
- felt
- glue in a squeeze bottle
- hole punches in a cup
- junk mail
- mailing labels
- markers
- paper plates
- paper scraps in a shoebox
- paste, in a jar lid
- pompoms
- quality plastic scissors
- ribbon
- sticky dot stickers
- white and construction paper
- yarn pieces

Prepare (Adult)

- Cover a low table with newspaper.
- Place a few of the materials in suitable containers on the table within easy reach of the children. Good containers vary according to what they hold, but some good ideas are shoeboxes, shoebox lids, margarine cups, coffee cans, plastic or wicker baskets, cardboard boxes, plastic bowls, or plastic storage containers.
- Sit back, observe, and enjoy the children's explorations!

Process (Child)

- The toddlers and twos:
  - Play freely and manipulate the art materials
  - Explore how art materials react
  - Discover how to control art materials
  - Enjoy their artistic efforts

Tips

- Begin with only one or two collage items, such as a container of cotton balls or sponge scraps. Add more choices as children become experienced.
- Toddlers and twos love to do art "by myself!" with complete freedom and without constraints.
- Do not be surprised if toddlers and twos:
  - Dip a marker into glue and try to draw with it
  - Shake all the glitter into the bowl of paint

- Put stickers on their arms
- Feel, smell, see, hear, and sometimes taste materials
- What an opportunity for toddlers and twos to find out what happens when they experiment and explore in ways that are new to them!
- Arrange materials in a clean and inviting way to encourage toddlers and twos to use the materials. Keep the area tidy, neat, and attractive. Toddlers and twos like to make a bit of a mess, but they do not like to sit down in front of one!

Variations

For a messier version of experimenting with process, add these supplies and materials:

- A puddle of paint in a pie tin
- Paintbrushes
- Water in a shallow dish
- Eyedroppers
- A ball of playclay or playdough

CHAPTER 1

Primarily Paint

Toddlers and twos are becoming independent thinkers who like to discover and explore on their own. "By myself" and "Me do it!" are common mantras of the toddler or two-year-old in action. They may be beginners, but they are ready to jump in all the way. Young children are explorers on an adventure in the new, exciting land of experiences, discovering paint and its possibilities and outcomes. One of the best aspects of paint is that it takes little effort to cover a large area (children like "big"). Also, children can easily make bright marks without using heavy pressure or needing great strength.

Toddlers and twos enjoy *using paint* more than creating a finished painting. Never before has the statement "It's the process, not the product" been truer or more obvious than when toddlers and twos use paint. They like to layer paint, mix colors until no recognizable color is left, discover how a brush works, and explore the mysteries of what paint can and cannot do. The adult's job is to just let it happen by providing a wide and varied range of supplies for the child and by simply enjoying the child's leap into the process of art exploration. Be prepared to assist with carrying wet paintings to a drying area, keeping sponges and buckets of soapy water handy, and keeping a stack of paper ready and waiting. There is no right or wrong way to paint—only the child's way!

First Fingerpainting

Fingerpainting is "the" classic painting experience for children. Slick, cool, and gooey, fingerpaint is a fun (and important) sensory activity for children to explore with their bare hands, spreading and smearing it on paper, discovering designs created by fingernails, fingertips, and palms.

Fingerpaint Recipes

Premixed Liquid Starch Fingerpaint
Premix ½ cup (120 mL) liquid starch and ½ cup (120 mL) liquid tempera paint in a cup. Spoon the mixture onto paper for fingerpainting.

Easiest Fingerpaint (child-made)
Pour a puddle of liquid starch on a piece of paper, and then squirt one or two tablespoons (15–30 mL) of liquid tempera paint onto the puddle. Encourage the child to mix the paint with his hands by spreading it around and fingerpainting with it.

Warm Cornstarch Fingerpaint
Dissolve 1 cup (240 mL) cornstarch into ½ cup (120 mL) cold water, and set aside. Boil 3 cups (720 mL) water in a saucepan on a stove or hot plate (adult only). Remove the pan from the heat, and add the cornstarch mixture to the hot water, stirring constantly. Place the pan back on the stove, and boil the mixture for about one minute, until clear and thick. Add ½ teaspoon (2 mL) food coloring. (Make sure the cornstarch is dissolved before adding this, or the mixture will be lumpy.) Allow the paint to cool down; encourage the children to paint with the warm (not hot) paint.

Creamy Soap Flake Fingerpaint
Pour 2 cups (480 mL) warm water in a bowl. Add 1 cup (240 mL) soap flakes, and beat with an electric mixer until stiff. Mix in ½ teaspoon (2 mL) food coloring. Spoon the paint onto paper for fingerpainting. (Make sure you use safe soap flakes such as Dreft™ or Ivory Snow™, and not regular laundry detergent. You can also grate a bar of Ivory Soap to make your own flakes.) Do not dump unused paint in the sink because it can clog the drain.

Easy Cleanup Tempera Fingerpaint
Mix ¼ cup (60 mL) tempera paint with ⅛ cup (30 mL) liquid soap. Spoon the mixture onto a piece of paper for fingerpainting.

Materials
fingerpaint (see the five recipes on the previous page)
masking tape
measuring cups and spoons
mixing spoons
old plastic tablecloth, shower curtain, or newspaper
white paper (glossy or shiny is best)

Prepare (Adult)

- Cover a low table with newspaper, a plastic tablecloth, or an old shower curtain.
- Tape a piece of white paper to the covered work surface.
- The best part: choose and prepare a fingerpaint recipe with the child's help.
- When the child is finished making a fingerpainting, transfer it to a drying area and allow it to dry completely.

Process (Child)

- Drop a puddle of paint in the middle of a piece of paper.
- Spread the paint around with hands, elbows, and fingers.
- Wash and dry hands anytime. (Children may want to do this frequently. Some prefer a damp towel or sponge to wipe paint off their hands.)

Fingerpaint Tools

> chopsticks
> comb
> cookie cutters (for stamping)
> drinking straws
> feather
> fork
> hair curler, any type
> pizza cutter or pastry cutter
> plastic margarine lid, cut in half
> small rolling pin
> spatula
> toy parts
> wooden salad fork

Tips

- Some children may hesitate about covering their hands with paint. If so, encourage them to explore the paint with their fingertips first. Other children, however, love to cover their hands with paint and wash them repeatedly.
- It's easier to carry the painting to a drying area if you place the fingerpainting paper on an open sheet of newspaper.
- If the fingerpainting curls when dry, iron it with an old iron set on warm. Cover the fingerpainting with a plain sheet of newsprint or an old towel to protect the iron.

Tabletop Fingerpainting

Fingerpainting directly on a tabletop surface is smooth, messy fun! Use this Dollar-Wise Slippery Fingerpaint recipe—it's fun to use and easy to clean up!

Materials

bowls

cornstarch

Dollar-Wise Slippery Tabletop Fingerpaint (or use any favorite fingerpaint mixture, see page 18)

fingerpainting tools (see list)

low table (on which to paint)

measuring cups

saucepan and mixing spoon

small plastic, paper, or foam cups, in a variety of sizes

stove or hot plate (adult only)

tempera paints

unflavored gelatin

water (cold, room temperature, and boiling)

Fingerpainting Tools

cardboard with masking tape around the edges

comb

empty yogurt container

plastic knife

plastic lid cut in half, then the straight edge cut into zigzags and waves

plastic-coated spatula

wooden spoon

Prepare (Adult)

- Make the Dollar-Wise Slippery Tabletop Fingerpaint recipe with the children. In a saucepan, mix ½ cup (60 g) cornstarch and ¾ cup (180 mL) cold water, and stir until smooth. Pour ¼ cup (60 mL) water into a small bowl, and add an envelope of gelatin. Set it aside until the gelatin dissolves slightly. Pour two cups (480 mL) boiling water into the saucepan mixture and stir. Place the saucepan on a stove or hot plate (adult only), and turn the heat on medium. Stir the cornstarch mixture constantly until it boils and becomes clear. Remove from heat. Add in the dissolved gelatin mixture and stir. When cool, pour it into separate bowls. Add a different color of tempera paint to each bowl.

- Place a variety of cups and fingerpainting tools on a low table.

- Pour a small puddle of paint directly on the tabletop, using one or more colors.

Combine ½ cup cornstarch and ¾ cup cold water into a saucepan. Stir until smooth.

Pour two cups of boiling water into saucepan mixture and stir!

Process (Child)

- Fingerpaint directly on the table with fingers and hands, smearing the paint smooth, and then making designs in the paint.
- Explore adding more than one color on the tabletop at a time and mixing them together.
- Experiment with various tools to make additional fingerpainting designs. For example, show children how to turn a small plastic or paper cup upside down and scoot the cup along the table, scraping the paint off wherever it goes and leaving a trail of clean space behind it. (This trail is called *negative space*.)

When cool, pour into separate bowls. Add a different color of tempera paint to each bowl.

Tips

- For their first experience, let children fingerpaint without any tools.
- If the paint begins to dry out on the table, add a spritz of water, a puddle of liquid starch, or more paint.
- Clean-up tip: Cut a plastic lid (e.g., from a margarine tub) in half, and use it as a scraper to scoop the paint off the table. Children love to explore the paint with this homemade scraper!

Variation

- Paint-and-Wash Art: Mix ½ cup (120 mL) tempera paint with 1 teaspoon (5 mL) liquid soap, and paint directly on a sliding glass door. Then, for the best part, ask the children to "wash" it off using a squeegee, a dishpan of warm soapy water, and old towels. It's messy, but it's fun!

Out & About Water Painting

Paint outside on rocks, fences, and sidewalks using just a paintbrush and a bucket of plain water. This is an easy project that requires little or no preparation or cleanup! Children love the industrious freedom of painting anywhere without worry. A child's work is never done!

Materials
old, fat paintbrushes
small bucket of water (a sandbox bucket or pail with a handle is perfect)

Prepare (Adult)
- Fill a small bucket with clear water, about ¼ full.

Process (Child)
- Plunk a fat paintbrush into the bucket.
- Paint with water on anything and everything! Toddlers and twos love to paint windows. The following are other favorite choices for this age group:
  - Painting lines, dots, and wiggles on a cement patio or sidewalk
  - Painting a wood fence or wall, rocks, trikes, swing sets, and outdoor toys

Tips
- Fill buckets less than half full so children can carry them around. (Carrying buckets of water is a new skill for most children.)
- A large plastic soda or liter bottle is a good container for children to "hug-carry." Cut away the spout of the bottle, and then pour about 1" (3 cm) water into it. Children also enjoy carrying cups with handles and using slightly smaller brushes.

Variations
- Paint with water using a variety of painting tools (see list).
- Paint river rocks. When the rocks dry, paint them again.
- Draw outdoors with chalk. Then paint on top of the chalk lines with water to blur or fill in the lines.

Painting Tools
broom or mop
dish mop with handle
feather duster
old sponge
paint roller
sponge brush

Story
One day Ned's mom dipped a brush in water and traced Ned's outline on the sidewalk. When Ned squatted beside his outline and tried to paint the traced area with more water, the lines kept evaporating before his eyes. He continued tracing and filling in the lines until he realized how water behaves at times. Children learn—and remember—best by doing.

First Color Mixing

Mixing colored water in the compartments of a plastic ice cube tray allows children to experiment with colors for the first time and to make new colors. Start with the three primary colors to make any hue under the rainbow!

3 compartments with colored water

Materials

ice cube tray
paintbrush
three small containers or plastic bowls (white or clear show colors best)
water
yellow, red, and blue food coloring

Prepare (Adult)

- Fill each compartment of a plastic ice cube tray half full with water.
- Put several drops of yellow food coloring into one of the compartments, several drops of red into another, and several drops of blue into another. Leave the rest of the sections with clear water only.
- Fill the three small containers with clear water, and set them aside.
- Place a paintbrush next to the ice cube tray.
- Put the food coloring bottles on the table to the side.
- Put several drops of food coloring into each of the water-filled small containers, and place them next to the ice cube tray (Adult).

Process (Child)

- Dip a paintbrush into the different compartments of the ice cube tray, and mix and explore the colors.
- Add the colors from the containers into the ice cube tray compartments for new shades and color mixing experiments.

Variations

- Freeze the full ice cube tray to see what the colors look like in solid form.
- Fill the ice cube tray with a mixture of cornstarch and water to make interesting pastel and opaque colors.
- Mix together water, liquid soap, and powdered tempera paint, and pour it into a plastic ice cube tray. Press a cork into each section, and freeze overnight. The cork will form a chubby handle. (Use leftover paint from the easel to make good use of old paint.)

Story

Giselle and Misty were painting with frozen balls of ice made from frozen water balloons. The frozen balloon balls were rolling around in the plastic tub, giving them the giggles and making their hands cold. Giselle said, "Wait." She wiped her hands on her art shirt and walked over to the dress-up corner where she found a glove and a mitten. She returned to the frozen painting activity and gave Misty the mitten, and put the glove on her own hand. Then they returned to their painting explorations, very pleased with themselves.

Paper Stain Painting

Painting without paint is a magical surprise for children. All you need is some crepe paper leftover from a birthday party and a little water.

Roll streamers into tight "sticks"

Tape to hold

Materials

crepe paper streamer, any color
dish
paper
scissors, optional
tape
water

Prepare (Adult)

- Roll a streamer of crepe paper into a tight "stick" or tube shape, and then tape it together on one end. The crepe paper stick should be about the size of a fat crayon.
- Place a sheet of paper on the worktable, and put a dish of plain water next to it. Place the crepe paper stick next to the dish. If you have more than one color of crepe paper, make as many stick rolls as you like.

Process (Child)

- Dip the crepe paper stick into the water, and "paint" with it on the plain paper. The color dye from the crepe paper will stain the paper.
- If the roll gets too soggy, snip off the end. Continue to dip the new edge into water.

Tip

- Crepe paper color is very bright and can stain fingers. It washes off within a few days.

Variation

- Roll up a piece of art tissue. Dip the end into water, and rub it on a piece of paper. Or moisten the paper first, and then color over it with a rolled-up piece of art tissue.
- Tear scraps of art tissue into big pieces. Place the pieces on a sheet of paper, paint over them with water, and then peel them off. The art tissue will leave stained designs on the paper. Or, leave the scraps on the paper to dry.

Story

Cam was very impressed that he could paint in a new way, using neither a brush nor his hands. After dipping crepe paper into water and then drawing it across his paper numerous times, Cam pulled off a corner of newspaper and dipped it into water to see if it would paint, too. Good thinking and experimenting, Cam!

Marvelous Homemade Paints—22 Recipes

The ingredients for a treasure of paint mixtures are right around the corner in the kitchen, laundry, and bath! Children will be intrigued, challenged, and delighted by painting with mixtures made from soap, flour, corn syrup, and other marvelous ingredients. Try these recipes any time, or when something new and different sounds like fun.

Materials
(see materials for each recipe)

Cold Cream Paint

cold cream
cornstarch
food coloring
measuring spoons
muffin tin with 6 sections
paintbrush
water

In each cup of a six-sectioned muffin tin, put 1 teaspoon (3 g) cornstarch, ½ teaspoon (3 g) cold cream, and ½ teaspoon (2 mL) water. Use a paintbrush to stir a different food coloring into each cup. Use as you would any paint. This also works as a gentle face paint.

1 teaspoon cornstarch

1/2 teaspoon cold cream

1/2 teaspoon water

Cornstarch Paint

cornstarch
liquid tempera paint
measuring cup
spoon and bowl

Mix 1 cup (240 mL) liquid tempera paint and 1 cup (125 g) cornstarch in a bowl to make a thick paint that sticks well to paper.

Corn Syrup & Food Coloring Paint

corn syrup
cup and spoon
food coloring

Pour 1 cup corn syrup into a cup, and mix in enough food coloring to make a bright color. Paint on white paper. The painting dries to a shiny but sticky result.

Cornstarch Vinegar Paint

cornstarch
food coloring
measuring cups and spoons
spoon and bowl or baby food jar with lid
white vinegar

Mix together 2 teaspoons (10 mL) white vinegar, 2 teaspoons (7 g) cornstarch, and 20 drops of food coloring (more or less is fine) in a bowl (or shake in a baby food jar). This makes enough paint for one child.

Egg Paint

bowl and fork
colored chalk (bright pastel chalk)
1 egg
muffin tin
old ceramic (or metal) bowl
paintbrush
round rock
spoon
teaspoon
water

Grind bits of chalk into a fine powder with a rock...

Break pieces of chalk and put them into an old ceramic or metal bowl. Grind them into powder using a round rock. Spoon the powder into muffin tin cups. Separate an egg. Set aside the egg white and put the yolk into a bowl with 2 teaspoons (10 mL) water. Whip the egg yolk and water with a fork until it is frothy yellow. Add drops of egg-water to the ground chalk. Stir with a paintbrush until the mixture is a smooth, thin paint.

Add egg water to the ground colored chalk... Stir for thin smooth paint!

Flour Paint

bowl or large jar
flour
food coloring drops or paste,
   or powdered tempera paint
liquid soap
measuring spoons and cups
spoon
water

Combine 3 cups (375 g) flour, 2 tablespoons (30 mL) liquid soap, and ¾ cup (180 mL) water in a bowl or large jar until the mixture is a thick paste. Mix in food color until the desired shade is reached.

Fragrant Paint

fragrances and spices (see suggestions below)
paint
spoon

Add fragrances and scents to paint. Some suggestions are shampoo; lemon, almond, or peppermint extract; scented hand lotion; perfume or cologne; fruit drink mix; chocolate powder; and coffee. Adding spices adds texture and fragrance. Suggestions include cloves, nutmeg, cinnamon, basil, and sage.

Frozen Liquid Watercolors

freezer
liquid watercolors
plastic spoons
small paper cups

Pour liquid watercolors into small paper cups, and put them into the freezer. When the liquid watercolors are partially frozen put plastic spoons into each cup. After the liquid watercolors freeze, remove the paper cups. The spoons become handles.

Jell-O™ Paint

bowl and spoon or jar with tight-fitting lid
gelatin powder
water

Add water to any gelatin powder, such as Jell-O™, so it has the consistency of watercolor paint. Use as a fingerpaint or a paint for brushing on glossy paper, freezer paper, or fingerpainting paper. This paint is great for "scratch & sniff."

Milk Paint

powdered milk
cornstarch
measuring cups and spoons
bowl and spoon
warm water
food coloring drops or food coloring paste

Mix together ½ cup (75 g) powdered milk and 2 teaspoons (7 g) cornstarch in a bowl. Gradually add in ½ cup (120 mL) warm water until the paint is smooth. Then add in food coloring.

Milk & Food Coloring Paint

bowl and spoon or jar with tight-fitting lid
food coloring
milk

Mix milk and food coloring together in a bowl or in a jar with a tight-fitting lid. Use as a paint for toast, bread, cupcakes, or other edible painting projects.

Mud Paint

cup
paintbrush
sifted soil
water

Mix sifted soil and water in a cup, stirring with a brush. Use it to paint on paper, fabric, or wood.

Paste Paint

flour
food coloring or tempera paint
measuring cups
saucepan and mixing spoon
stove or hot plate (adult only)
water

Mix together 1 cup (125 g) flour and 3 cups (720 mL) water in a saucepan. Boil on a stove or hot plate until the mixture is thick (adult step). Mix in any coloring, such as tempera paint or food coloring, for a paint that will keep its texture when it dries.

Shampoo Paint

bowl and spoon
electric mixer
food coloring, optional
measuring spoon
shampoo
water

Mix 3 teaspoons (30 g) shampoo with a little water in a bowl, and then whip with an electric mixer until it is thick and creamy. If desired, add food coloring.

Shaving Cream & Glue Paint

bowl and mixing spoon
food coloring
measuring cup
shaving cream
white glue

Mix 1 cup (30 g) shaving cream with 1 cup (240 mL) white glue in a bowl. Add in food coloring as desired. This makes a puffy paint that works well on cardboard or paper.

Shiny Milk Paint

jar with tight-fitting lid
sweetened condensed milk
tempera paint

Mix together ¼ can sweetened condensed milk with enough tempera paint to make a bright color in a jar with a tight-fitting lid. Repeat

mixing three more colors with the rest of the milk, ¼ can milk each. When the paint dries, it will be shiny.

Slick Paint

bowl and spoon
tempera paint
white glue

Stir together an equal amount of tempera paint and white glue in a bowl. This mixture works well on glass and other slick surfaces like aluminum foil.

Milk Paint

powdered milk
cornstarch
measuring cups and spoons
bowl and spoon
warm water
food coloring drops or food coloring paste

Mix together ½ cup (75 g) powdered milk and 2 teaspoons (7 g) cornstarch in a bowl. Gradually add in ½ cup (120 mL) warm water until the paint is smooth. Then add in food coloring.

Tea Paint

bowl or cup

measuring cup

tea bag or instant coffee

water

Soak a tea bag in ¼ cup (60 mL) water, or add instant coffee to the water. Make it dark or light, for color variation. Use this paint on plain paper or for shading.

Tempera & Starch Brush On

bowl and spoon

liquid starch

measuring cups

tempera paint

water

Mix together 2 cups (480 mL) tempera paint and 1 cup (240 mL) liquid starch in a bowl until it is smooth and creamy. Add water slowly while mixing, until the paint is thick and spreadable. Use it for painting on any type of paper, cardboard, or wood.

Textured Paint

spoon

tempera paint

textures (see suggestions below)

Add textures to tempera paints (or any of the paint mixtures in this book). Some texture possibilities are coffee grounds, sand, salt, sawdust, pencil shavings, oatmeal, or crumbled leaves.

Vinegar Watercolor Paint

baking soda

cornstarch

glycerin

liquid food coloring

measuring spoons

plastic bottle caps from 2-liter bottles

small bowl and spoon

white vinegar

Mix together 1 tablespoon (15 mL) white vinegar and 2 tablespoons (30 g) baking soda in a small bowl; it will bubble. When it stops bubbling, add 1 tablespoon (10 g) cornstarch and ¼ teaspoon (1 mL) glycerin, mixing well. Pour the mixture into bottle caps. Add several drops of food coloring to each bottle cap. Allow it to dry overnight to make a watercolor paint similar to those found in watercolor paint boxes. (Double or triple this recipe to make more colors or to fill more caps.)

Painting Goes Wild!

Collect and create homemade paintbrushes using imaginative materials such as feathers, bristles taped together, fern leaves, a sponge on a stick, or cattails. Each adds surprise to a painting experiment.

Materials

foam grocery trays

homemade brushes (see list)

newspaper or a plastic tablecloth

paper, in a variety of sizes and types

tempera paints

tray

Things to Use as Homemade Brushes

broom bristles (break a few bristles off an outdoor broom, and tape together)

cattails with long stems

fern leaves

inflated balloons

long feathers

pine branches with needles attached

small sponges clipped in a clothespin or tied to the end of a chopstick

sock or mitten on one hand

Prepare (Adult)

- Protect the work area with newspaper or a plastic tablecloth.
- Place several colors of tempera paints into foam grocery trays, and put them on the table. Tape them to the table, if needed.
- Place a sheet of paper in front of each toddler.
- Put several types of homemade brushes on a tray from which children can choose.

Process (Child)

- Dip a homemade paintbrush into paint, then brush the paint on the paper.
- Try other brushes as desired.
- Paint with homemade brushes at the easel, on paper on the floor, or on paper taped to the wall.

Tip

- Place a loop of masking tape on the bottom of each paint tray to keep it attached to the table. Sometimes the homemade brushes can stick to the paint and lift the trays if they are not taped.

Tempera Dabble

For a uniquely fundamental painting experience, dab a cotton ball into dry tempera paint, and rub it on paper. Then brush over the dry tempera paint marks with water. Children are very interested in the dry, soft powdery paint.

Materials

cotton balls

cup

large plastic or metal lids, one for each color

newspaper or plastic tablecloth, if needed

paintbrush

powdered tempera paints

spoon

water

white paper

Prepare (Adult)

- Cover a table with newspaper or a plastic tablecloth, if needed.
- Spoon about ½ teaspoon (2 g) powdered tempera paint into each jar lid, one color per lid.
- Place one cotton ball into each lid. Place the lids next to a sheet of white paper.
- Pour 1" (3 cm) water into a cup, and place it next to the paper.

Process (Child)

- Press a cotton ball into dry tempera paint, and then dab or rub it on the paper.
- To brighten the colors, dip a paintbrush into the cup of water, and paint over the dry tempera design. Watch the colors blend together. (Children can also dab a clean cotton ball or cotton swab in the water and brush it through the dry paint on the paper.)

Tips

- Children can explore mixing water and paint in the lid. Or they can try out other ideas of their own. Encourage creativity. Do not be surprised when children dip cotton balls into the water and the paintbrush into the powdered paint.
- To reduce the problem of puffs of powdery paint being inhaled, spray the child's paper with water before dabbing on the powdered paint. Some children think it is fun to wear paint filter masks from the hardware store, but this is not necessary.

Variation

- Sprinkle dry powdered tempera paint on a piece of paper or cardboard, and carry it out into the rain. The raindrops will turn the powdered paint into wet colors.

Paint It: Four Process Ideas

Discovering different ways of painting is exciting for children. Just when they think they've tried it all, another new way to paint surfaces. The following four approaches to painting are particularly popular with children and easy for adults to prepare. Try one, or try them all!

Roly-Poly It

Materials
large paper
paint rollers, different sizes
paint trays or old cookie sheets
tape
tempera paint

Prepare (Adult)
- Pour puddles of tempera paint onto trays or old cookie sheets.
- Tape a large piece of paper to the table or on a wall.
- Put out a variety of paint rollers.

Process (Child)
- Roll real paint rollers through the paint and then onto big paper that has room to experiment and explore. Use small cylinder or foam covered paint rollers (toddlers and twos seem to like the small rollers best).

Tip
- Soak used paint rollers in a bucket of water for easy cleanup, or freeze in a plastic bag for use the next day.

Variation
- Tape a piece of large paper to a fence. When the child rolls the paint roller over it, the rollers and paint will pick up the fence pattern from underneath.

Story
Fritz was having the most enjoyable time walking around his table with a huge grin on his face, repeatedly rolling his paint roller the entire time. Sometimes he rolled his roller without paint and sometimes with it. Rolling in any fashion seemed to be the important component for Fritz.

Ribbon It

Materials
paper
ribbons
scissors
tempera paint
wet paper towels or sponges
yarn, string, jewelry chains, or strings of
    beads, optional

Prepare (Adult)
- Cut ribbons into 1'–2' (30 cm–60 cm)
  lengths, and place them on the table.
- Pour puddles of paint on a tray or on a
  newspaper-covered table.
- Keep wet paper towels or sponges nearby
  for wiping painted fingers and hands.

Process (Child)
- Drop the ribbons into a puddle of paint,
  use hands to stir and coat them, and then
  drop them on a piece of paper to make
  curly patterns and prints.
- Drop, drag, or wiggle a ribbon on the
  paper, making one or more wiggly
  patterned paintings.
- Experiment with yarn, string, or even
  jewelry chains and strings of beads, if
  desired.

Absorb It

Materials
bucket of water
coffee filters
misting spray bottle, optional
newspaper
paintbrushes
water in cups
water-based markers

Prepare (Adult)
- Place open, flat coffee filters on a piece of
  newspaper.
- Put out water-based markers, cups of
  water, and paintbrushes.

Process (Child)
- Draw with the markers on a coffee filter,
  and then paint the marker lines with a
  paintbrush dipped in water.
- The marker lines come to life, blurring and
  spreading into the absorbent coffee filter—
  a magical and beautiful sight!

Variations
- Draw with the markers as above, but spray
  the filter with a misting spray bottle filled
  with water.
- Dab the marker lines with a wet sponge.

Puff It

Materials

food coloring or liquid watercolors
infant nasal syringe or turkey baster, optional
large pin (adult only)
paper
spoons
straws
tray or cookie sheet
water

Prepare (Adult)

- Use a large pin to poke holes into a plastic drinking straw. This prevents children from sucking paint up the straw, but not from blowing air out.
- Pour ¼ cup (60 mL) water into a cup, and add 2 teaspoons (10 mL) food coloring or liquid watercolors.
- Spoon a small puddle of the colored water on a sheet of paper on a tray or cookie sheet.

Process (Child)

- Point the straw at the puddle of colored water, and blow through the straw. Watch the color run and spray in different directions.
- Turn the tray, and blow again to encourage the paint to spray and flow.
- For other puffy air painting, squeeze a baby nasal syringe to puff the paint on the paper. Try a turkey baster, too. Empty spray bottles also will provide puffs of air.

Story

The first time Meg and Ivy tried blowing paint on paper with straws, they did not realize the straws had been prepared with holes to prevent the paint from being inhaled. And like most children, they sucked in instead of blowing out! When sucking in did not do anything to the paint, they both "blew out" and were delighted to make their paint shoot out in wonderful spidery designs! Good adult preparation helps children learn as they experience.

Magic Paint Bag

Fill a heavy-duty zipper-closure bag with a few tablespoons of paint, and "draw" designs on the bag that are easily erased and drawn again (similar to a "magic slate"). Wherever the bag is pressed with a finger, the paint is displaced, and the paper underneath shows through.

Zip closed after squeezing out the air...

Materials

blunt drawing tools, such as fingers, wooden craft sticks, or spoons
large, heavy-duty, plastic zipper-closure bag
masking tape
measuring spoon
tempera paint, in thick, dark colors
white paper, about 8 ½" x 11" (21 cm x 27 cm)

Prepare (Adult)

- Spoon 3 tablespoons (45 mL) tempera paint into a heavy-duty plastic bag. Ease out as much air as possible, and then zip the bag closed. (Children will enjoy helping.)
- Place white paper (slightly smaller than the size of the bag) on a low table, and put the paint-filled bag on top of it.
- Tape the edges of the bag to the table.

Process (Child)

- Smooth the paint into a thin layer inside the bag using a flat hand.

- Rub fingertips over the flat side of the bag to draw lines and scribbles, and experiment with other blunt tools such as a wooden craft stick or spoon. The paper will show through.
- Wipe away the designs by gently rubbing hands over the bag, and then start again.

Tips

- Children enjoy spooning the paint into the baggie.
- A freezer bag is quite strong, and children do not usually tear through the baggie with their nails. However, if you are concerned about leaking paint, double the bag.

Variations

- Fill the bags with other colorful ingredients, such as blue hair gel or liquid starch tinted with food coloring.
- Slip a sheet of aluminum foil into the bag, and place the paint on top of the foil. Close the bag, and draw on the surface as above. The foil will show through.

Place bag on sheet of paper... Tape edges to the table

Texture Scrap Painting

Children are often interested in painting on their actual clothing, so painting on fabric scraps or old, worn clothes is a new, real-life experiment without the concerns of ruining favorite outfits.

Materials
fabric paints, optional
newspapers or plastic tablecloth
old fabric-sample book (from an upholstery, furniture, or drapery store) or old, worn-out clothing
paintbrush
pie tin or small tray
tempera paints, one or more colors

Prepare (Adult)
- Cover a low table with newspapers or a plastic tablecloth.
- Take apart the fabric-sample book, and place several squares of fabric with differing textures on the table. Or cut some of the child's favorite old worn-out dresses or play clothes into squares. Children may wish to help choose scraps.
- Pour a puddle of tempera paint (or several puddles of different colors) into a pie tin or on a small tray, and rest a paintbrush in the paint.

Process (Child)
- Brush paint on the fabric squares.
- Notice how the paint acts on different textures.

Tips
- Children like to handle and explore the fabrics before painting on them.
- Tempera paint tends to flake off fabric once it dries, so this project is not permanent unless you substitute fabric paints. The value of this project is the process more than the finished product.

Variations
- Use permanent fabric paint to paint on a white tablecloth to use for picnics. (Make sure the children wear art clothes for this variation, because permanent fabric paint will stain everything!)
- Spread an old sheet or piece of muslin on the ground or on a table, and paint directly on it like paper.

Story
Michaela and her mom made a quilt out of Michaela's favorite outgrown play clothes and her custom-painted fabric squares. It has become their family's treasured traditional picnic quilt. Michaela can see her favorite daisy dress and pastel baby undershirt stitched right into the quilt—a topic of conversation each time they unfold it for a picnic. Michaela always wants to sit on the square made from her old jeans with the little embroidered flowers on the pocket. It's her special picnic square!

Paper Quilt Painting

Tape together different kinds of papers to make a giant paper "quilt" on which to paint. Children will enjoy the different textures, and they may notice how the papers react, attracting or resisting paint.

Materials

different types of paper in similar sizes (see list)
paintbrush
shallow dish
tape
tempera paint (one or many colors)

Different Types of Paper

butcher
construction
foil
grocery bag
newspaper
old poster
paper towel
parchment
wallpaper
wax paper
wrapping paper
wrinkled newsprint

Prepare (Adult)

- Tape together all the chosen sheets of papers to make a giant paper quilt that covers a child-height table.
- Tape down the corners of the paper quilt to prevent wiggly paper.
- Pour tempera paint into a shallow dish, and place a paintbrush in the middle of it. Use several dishes of colors, if desired.

Process (Child)

- Paint anywhere on the paper quilt.
- Observe how the paint looks different on absorbent papers such as construction paper versus resistant papers such as foil or waxed paper.

Tips

- The first time you do this activity, make a quilt with only a few squares. Gradually move to larger quilts with more squares as children gain skill or progress to working on the floor.
- Alternate idea: Paint the papers first, and then tape them together into a quilt pattern.

Story

Megan was painting her quilt with red sunburst circles on each square. She repeated the same design over and over, fascinated that each kind of paper caused the paint to act differently. While some children might find this a bit frustrating, Megan found it intriguing and explored the possibilities quietly and deep in thought.

Rainy Day Spray

Shower curtains are meant to be wet, so why not use one as a canvas for rainy artwork?

Materials

empty, clean spice shaker jars or salt and
    pepper jars
old plastic shower curtain
powdered tempera paint
rainy day (if there is no rain, fill a misting
    bottle with water)
scissors
shoebox or basket

Prepare (Adult)

- Wait to do this activity outdoors on a
  mildly rainy day (no big wind, and no
  thunder and lightning!). Wear any rain gear
  necessary.
- Cut a shower curtain into individual
  squares that a child can carry, perhaps
  12" x 12" (30 cm x 30 cm).
- Put different colors of powdered tempera
  paints into empty spice shakers or salt and
  pepper shakers.

- Place the shakers in a shoebox or basket
  for carrying.
- When done, help the children carry the art
  back inside, and let it dry.

Process (Child)

- Carry the plastic squares and paints
  outdoors.
- Place the squares on the grass or sidewalk.
- Sprinkle different colors of powdered
  tempera on the squares. (Drops of liquid
  tempera paint work, too.)
- Let the raindrops plop on the plastic,
  bringing the powdered paint to life. Colors
  will mix and blend on their own.

Tips

- Some children will find it easier to carry
  their plastic square on a cookie sheet or
  plastic tray.
- Do not be too surprised—most children
  want to put their fingers into the wet paint!

Story

Victoria and Robin had never worked on art projects in the rain before, so they were excited about preparing for the outdoor art adventure. Each girl placed her plastic square on a paper plate for easy carrying, and then sprinkled her square with multiple colors of powdered paint from spice shakers. Then came the adventure! Victoria and Robin carried their squares right out into the falling rain! As the drops hit their plastic and paint, they squealed with delight each time a drop hit a color of paint. They loved the magic of the dry, dull paint changing to wet and bright color right before their eyes.

CHAPTER 2

Hands on Dough

Playdough, clays, and other exploratory sensory mixtures are rich in open-ended possibilities for toddlers and twos. Stretch it this way, pound it that way, cut it, tear it, pour it, squeeze it, poke it, and sculpt it! Experience the moment! The finished product (if there is one) will not be as important as the process. Each doughlike recipe or squeezy material will produce an all-new and wondrous sensory experience for toddlers and twos. Do not be surprised if some children plunge both hands into playdough, while others are uncomfortable with the feeling of dough on their hands. Provide handy clean-up sponges or wet towels for easy hand wiping to encourage the reluctant child. Sometimes waiting a week or two and trying again is all it takes for children to decide they are ready to take the plunge!

Doughs and mixtures can be a calm, soothing experience or an exuberant active delight. The adult's role is to supervise closely and to bring out tools or put away materials when children need to increase or decrease their involvement. Sometimes toddlers and twos want to dry off, clean up, and move on to new activities, but they need the help of an adult to master the transition from something as exciting as mush or mud to something as calm as sharing a book. One final thought is so aptly stated by child development expert Clare Cherry in *Creative Art for the Developing Child: A Guide for Early Childhood Education*, "The finest experience that can be given a child with playdough is to let him make his own."

Cherry, Clare. 2001. *Creative art for the developing child: A guide for early childhood education.* Belmont, CA: Fearon.

Feelie Goop

Children love "touchy-feelie" tactile projects. Cornstarch mixed with water has wonderful and unique physical properties—gooey when poured from a spoon, but hard if squeezed in the hands. And the nice part is how easy it is to clean up with just water.

Materials

cornstarch
food coloring
heavy baking pan or plastic dishtub
old tablecloth or dishtowel, if needed
spoons, measuring cups, and other kitchen
   tools
water

Prepare (Adult)

- Premeasure 2 cups (250 g) cornstarch into a baking pan or plastic dishtub. Ask the children to help, if desired. If a child will be handling the dry cornstarch before adding water, place an old tablecloth or large dishtowel under the pan to help contain the powder that may puff out.
- Put the food coloring, spoons, measuring cups, and any other kitchen items on the table to use for exploring.
- Premeasure 1 cup (240 mL) of water, and set it aside.

Process (Child)

- Stand at the table, and feel the dry cornstarch with bare hands. (Standing works better than sitting for toddlers and twos.)
- Add water to the cornstarch, and mix it using bare hands. Feel the difference.
- Children love color! Squeeze drops of color from the little food coloring squeeze bottles. Add drops of two or more colors into the mixture, and mix with hands, watching as the colors swirl and blend.
- Explore the mixture with spoons, cups, or other kitchen items.

Tips

- Cornstarch is nontoxic, though not particularly appetizing. It will not harm children who cannot resist tasting it.
- Scrape dried drips off the floor with the edge of a dustpan, and sweep up.
- Add more cornstarch for a thicker mixture or more water for a runnier mixture.

Story

Lynn and Marsha, two child care providers, decided to try making feelie goop before giving it to the children, so they would know what it was all about, and to plan for discoveries and successful setup. Neither had made feelie goop before. After creating a batch, they began to pour it from one bowl to another. Jan, the center's teacher for school-age children, heard laughing and screaming coming from the toddler room and rushed over to see what was happening. She was surprised to see Lynn and Marsha having the times of their lives playing with goop that was at once solid and liquid. It did not take her long to get her hands into it, too!

Clean Mush

Most children have experimented with unrolling at least one roll of toilet paper into a big, soft pile of white ribbon! Finally, a project that not only allows for unrolling it, but for mixing and mooshing it into the most wonderful stuff! "Clean Mush" is a perfect name for this mixture.

Materials

bar of Ivory soap, grated

3 full rolls of toilet paper

measuring spoons and cups, mashers, and scoops, optional

old cheese grater

plastic container with lid, about the size of a storage container

warm water

Prepare (Adult)

- Grate a bar of Ivory soap using an old cheese grater.
- Put the rest of the materials on the worktable.

Process (Child)

- Unroll the toilet paper (with adult help). Put the toilet paper and grated soap into a large plastic container. Add enough warm water to saturate the mixture. Double or triple the recipe for even more fun!
- Mix it using bare hands.
- Squish, poke, pat, squeeze, and otherwise feel the wonderful clean mush. This is what sensory experiences are all about!

  Hint: This mixture will not harden into any shapes or lasting sculptures unless the water is squished out. The mixture will last less than a week (one or two days is average).

- If desired, add a few tools for exploring, such as measuring cups, spoons, mashers, and scoops.
- When finished, cleaning up is very easy. Just snap on the lid, or cover the container with plastic wrap, making an airtight seal.

Variations

- Place the rolls of toilet tissue on short dowels or sticks so the children can spin them to unroll the paper into a big, soft, fluffy pile on the floor.
- Make the mush in a sand and water table.
- Squish out the excess water, and use the mixture to mold sculptures somewhat like clay. Place each one on a piece of aluminum foil, and let them dry overnight.

Outdoor Mudpies

What is the point of being a child if you can't play with real mud? All you need is dirt and water and a little bit of patience and understanding. Children need no direction for this classic sensory experience.

Materials

appropriate clothing, such as a
   bathing suit or old play clothes
bucket, plastic dishpans, bowls,
   spoons, and cups
dirt
garden hose
shovel
warm day

Prepare (Adult)

- Help the children put on appropriate clothing for this activity, such as bathing suits or old play clothes.
- With the children's help, dig a hole in the dirt to loosen and soften the soil.
- Turn on the garden hose, and add water to the dirt.

Process (Child)

- Sit in the dirt, and mix and explore using hands and other tools and supplies.
- Simply hose off for easy cleanup! However, a warm and soapy bath or shower may still be necessary.

Tip

- Many toddlers and twos find dirty hands distasteful, especially if they are in their potty-training phase. If so, choose a different activity.

Variation

- *Indoor Mudpies*: Spread everything on a tarp on the floor with old towels nearby. Work with sifted "clean" dirt, free of rocks and twigs. Mix the dirt and water in a plastic tub.

Story

Megan and Julie wanted to make mudpies in the backyard one summer day. Megan's mother helped them get the hose and some spades and shovels for the area Mom felt was a good place for digging and playing. The girls dug a hole about 1' (30 cm) deep and 3' (90 cm) wide and called it "The Mud Pit." They filled it with thick mud made by squishing the dirt with water from the hose. Megan and Julie are now 24 years old, and they remember this as the most fun they ever had together in all their wonderful childhood days. Mom remembers that hosing them off did about half the clean-up job, while several warm soapy showers did the rest. Luckily the swimsuits they had been wearing were old ones—perfect for mud play.

Squeezing Rainbows

Squeeze and knead a plastic baggie filled with bright colors of partially set gelatin, and enjoy the feel and sight of thick colors blending.

Materials

heavy zipper-closure plastic baggie (freezer bag)
hot plate or stove (adult only)
masking tape
measuring cups
2 packages unflavored gelatin
red, yellow, and blue food coloring
3 small bowls
small saucepan
water
wooden spoon

Prepare (Adult)

- Prepare the rainbow gel. Stir 1½ cups (360 mL) water and 2 packages of gelatin in a small saucepan, and wait 5 minutes for the gelatin to soften. Stir over low heat for about 3 minutes or until the gelatin has dissolved. Remove from heat, and pour into three small bowls. Add 5 drops of food coloring to each bowl, and chill in refrigerator for about 10 minutes until partially set and thickened. Stir a few times while it chills. **Caution:** Supervise child-helpers closely.
- Spoon two or more colors into a heavy plastic zipper-closure baggie. The baggie does not need to be very full. (Children like to help with the spooning step.)
- Zip the bag closed. To help prevent leaks, tape the opening of the baggie with masking tape.
- Hand the baggie to the child.

Process (Child)

- Squeeze and knead this cool bag of colors. Discover how the colors mix together. Work at a table, on the floor, or on a lap. (This is fun for car rides or waiting times.)
- Empty the bag, and try mixing different colors together.

Tips

- Mix unflavored gelatin, such as Knox™, with food coloring to make a thick mixture with colors that blend slowly, allowing the child time to see the process.
- Most children find this activity soothing and calming.

Variation

- Place other materials or mixtures into a heavy baggie for children to explore, with or without coloring. The following are fun examples:
  - Equal parts water and cornstarch
  - Hair gel
  - Liquid starch
  - Shaving cream
  - Two or three flavors of bright fruit gelatin such as Jell-O™, no added color needed

Stretchy Dough

Soft and stretchy playdough has the texture and feel of comforting, soft, bread dough. Stir the ingredients together (no cooking needed), and make a big mound for pounding, squeezing, pulling apart, and poking.

Materials
art shirt or apron
Stretchy Dough Recipe
    flour
    food coloring
    measuring cups and spoons
    mixing bowl
    vegetable oil
    water
    wooden spoon and hands
tools for modeling and exploring the playdough (see list)

Sculpting Tools
chopsticks
dowels (for rolling)
drinking straws
forks
plastic knives
spatulas (for cutting)
spoons
wooden craft sticks
wooden stir sticks

Prepare (Adult)
- This dough is oily, so protect the table with a plastic tablecloth or work directly on the bare tabletop.
- Mix 1 cup (240 mL) oil, 1 cup (240 mL) water, and 1 teaspoon (5 mL) food coloring in a bowl. Slowly add in 4 cups (500 g) flour, and stir with a wooden spoon or hands until the dough forms a ball. Children like to help mix.
- Put the dough on the table, and knead until smooth. Children greatly enjoy the kneading process.

Process (Child)
- Help children put on art shirts or smocks because the dough is very oily.
- Pound, roll, knead, pull, poke, and stretch the dough.
- Add sculpting tools for exploration.
  Hint: This dough does not hold a shape well and is not meant for intricate sculpting projects.

Variation
- Make Fruity Playdough. Children love the fragrance and color of this dough. Do not worry about them eating it—one taste of the extremely salty dough, and they will avoid tasting it twice!

Fruity Playdough Recipe

cream of tartar

flour

measuring cups and spoons

mixing spoon

oil

package of unsweetened powdered fruit
   drink, such as Kool-Aid

salt

saucepan or electric fry pan (adult only)

stove or hot plate (adult only)

water

Mix 2 cups (250 g) flour, 4 tablespoons (60 g) cream of tartar, 2 cups water (480 mL), 2 tablespoons oil (30 mL), 1 cup salt (250 g), and a package of unsweetened powdered fruit drink in a saucepan or electric fry pan. Cook over medium heat until it forms a ball and has the consistency of playdough. Put the dough on a floured board or table, and knead until smooth. Children enjoy working with warm playdough. Otherwise, cool and store in a covered container.

Tips

- This playdough is easy to clean up because it sticks together and does not crumble. It is also a quick and easy playdough to use when in a hurry.
- Clean-up tip: Soak the tools in a dishtub of water. The dough will soften and dissolve easily.

Stir over medium heat 3 to 5 minutes.

1 tablespoon of oil

Then add...

2 tablespoons
Cream of Tartar

Mix these together

Story

Three children were playing with Stretchy Dough, each absorbed in his own discovery and experience. Max began pounding his ball of dough with his fist, and within seconds, Darien and Thomas were pounding away with identical grins on their faces. They were now one group together instead of three alone.

Rubbery Flubbery Dough

This soft, cooked dough has a rubbery feel, like a soft gumdrop. It is excellent for molding rolled shapes such as balls or coils, pleasing to poke things into, never crumbly, and especially wonderful to pound with a wooden toy mallet for a great release of energy!

Materials

airtight container or plastic bag
box lids
items to stick into dough (see list)
Rubbery Flubbery Dough
    cold water
    cornstarch
    hot water
    measuring cups
    mixing bowl and spoon
    salt
    saucepan and hot plate or stove (adult only)
wide dowel or rolling pin
wooden toy mallet or block of wood

Combine...

Items to Stick into Dough
- birthday candles
- chopsticks
- craft sticks
- golf tees
- large pegs
- plastic animals
- plastic or wooden stir sticks
- straws

Prepare (Adult)

- Make the dough. (Children love to help and particularly enjoy putting their hands in the soft cornstarch, but all steps involving heating and cooking are to be done by adults.) Pour 1 cup (125 g) cornstarch and ½ cup (120 mL) cold water into a mixing bowl, and stir with a spoon. Set it aside. Measure 1 cup (250 g) salt and 1 cup (240 mL) hot water into a saucepan on a hot plate or stove, and bring the mixture to a boil. Pour the contents of the mixing bowl into the hot saucepan mixture. Turn down the heat to low. Stir constantly while it cooks, until the mixture is dry and thick (like pie dough). Remove from the heat, and put the dough on a board or counter to cool. After it cools, knead until smooth. (Children love kneading warm dough!)
- Put out a toy mallet or block of wood, a rolling pin or dowel, and a selection of items (in box lids) for poking the dough.

Process (Child)

- Mold and squeeze the dough.
- Hammer the dough with a wooden toy mallet or block of wood. (Make sure the dough is on a surface that will not be damaged.)
- Choose tools for poking and pushing into the dough. Decorate the dough with as many items as desired. This dough will air-dry with the items sticking in it.

Tips

- Children with allergies will enjoy this wheat-free and gluten-free dough.
- If the dough gets sticky, pour some dry, powdery cornstarch on the table, and roll the dough in it (children love doing this).
- Although this recipe stores well in an airtight container, it does dry out more quickly than other playclay mixtures.
- To easily transport playclay sculptures, place them on a juice can lid or coffee can lid. Children can carry their own sculptures even if sculptures are not dry.

Pour contents of bowl into hot saucepan mixture...
Turn heat down low

Stir constantly

Knead until smooth!

Playclay

Squeeze, roll, cut, press, model, and play with this supersoft homemade playclay that is a delight to touch. There are many commercial playdoughs and homemade recipes that are too hard and stiff for the smallest hands to manipulate, but this one is great! A huge mound of this long-lasting dough is easy to handle.

Materials

airtight container or zipper-closure plastic bag
Playclay Recipe
    cream of tartar
    flour
    food coloring
    hot plate or stove (adult only)
    large saucepan
    measuring cups and spoons
    salt
    vegetable oil
    water
    wooden spoon
tools to use with playclay (see list)

Playclay Tools

    birthday candles
    cookie cutters, with handles
    feathers
    garlic press
    hair combs
    kitchen gadgets
    plastic knives
    plastic scissors
    potato mashers
    rolling piecrust or
        pastry cutter
    rolling pin
    small toy cars
    straws

Prepare (Adult)

- Prepare playclay (children love to help). Combine 5 cups (1.2 L) water, 2½ cups (625 g) salt, 3 tablespoons (45 g) cream of tartar, and food coloring (1 teaspoon for pastel color and 3 tablespoons for vivid color) in a large saucepan on a hot plate or stove (adult only). Cook on low heat, and stir with a wooden spoon. As the mixture heats up, stir in 10 tablespoons (150 mL) oil, and then 5 cups (625 g) flour slowly.

- Keep stirring until the mixture starts looking dry and pulls away from the sides of the pan. Remove the pan from the heat at this point. Pinch a piece between two fingers. If it is not sticky, it is done. Otherwise, continue stirring over heat.

- Place the dough on the counter, and knead until smooth. Children will enjoy kneading, too!

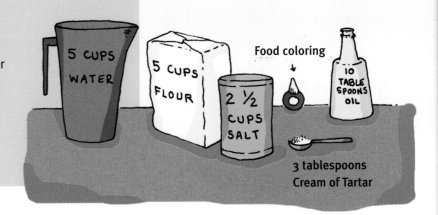

5 CUPS WATER
5 CUPS FLOUR
2 ½ CUPS SALT
Food coloring
10 TABLE SPOONS OIL
3 tablespoons Cream of Tartar

Process (Child)

- Knead the warm playclay.
- Model the playclay while it is still warm (but not hot!), exploring it with bare hands.
- Use a variety of tools and utensils on the dough:
  - Press the dough with a potato masher
  - Roll the dough flat with a rolling pin, and cut out "cookies"
  - Squeeze spaghetti-like strands with a garlic press
  - Roll long worm shapes, and cut them with a plastic knife or plastic scissors.
  - Poke the dough with candles and straws

The possibilities are infinite!

- When finished, store playclay in an airtight container or plastic bag, and reuse again and again. Do not refrigerate.

Variations

- Single "serving" recipe: Use 1 cup (240 mL) water, ½ cup (125 g) salt, 2 teaspoons (10 g) cream of tartar, ½ to 2 teaspoons (2 to 10 mL) food coloring, 2 tablespoons (30 mL) vegetable oil, and 1 cup (125 g) flour. Prepare the same way as the large batch.
- Cook two or more batches of playclay, each a different color, and mix them together.
- Add interesting fragrances or textures to playclay, such as shampoo, sand, perfume, almond or lemon or other extracts, and coffee grounds.

Keep stirring until mixture looks dry and pulls away from sides of pan...

Story

Cathryn was patting and forming her dough into at least 10 little cookie shapes. When she was done, she put her hands on her hips and said quietly to herself as she pointed to each one, "For Daddy, for Mommy, for Justin, for Ruffer, for Cathryn..." Sharing cookies is the best beginning mathematics experience. Cathryn was doing division!

Sculpture in a Bag

Squeezing plaster of Paris to make permanent sculptures is pure magic! First, it's squishy, and then it suddenly turns warm and solid. Science and art in one!

Place 2 or 3 colors of paint in a pan

Materials
paintbrush
plaster of Paris
shallow dish or pan
sturdy sandwich-sized baggies, twist-tie type
tempera paints
water

Prepare (Adult)
- Place two or three colors of paint into a shallow dish or pan, and put a paintbrush next to it. Set it aside.
- Measure 1 cup (125 g) plaster of Paris and ½ cup (120 mL) water into the sandwich baggie. Children like to help with measuring.
- Use a twist tie (or zipper closure) to close the bag, expelling as much air as possible.
- Hand the baggie to the toddler.
- Remove the plastic bag after the plaster of Paris has hardened (it takes only a few minutes). Inside the bag will be the child's unique hand-formed sculpture.

Process (Child)
- Squeeze, knead, push, and poke the bag. As the plaster and water mix, the contents of the bag will harden into a shape.
- Remove the shape from the bag (Adult).
- Paint dry sculptures with the tempera paints. (Mix the colors in the dish first, or blend them together on the sculpture.) Allow the paint to dry.

Tips
- Because children may use energetic mixing styles, double-bag the plaster.
- Use less or more of the mixture in the baggie to make it easier or harder to squish the mixture around inside. Each will create a different sculpture when dry.

Variation
- For pastel-tinted sculptures, add watercolor paints, food coloring, or tempera paints to ½ cup (120 mL) water, and mix it into the dry plaster.

Story
Kimmy and Lana were working together making plaster sculptures, happily squeezing the squishy liquid plaster. All of a sudden, as if on cue, their eyes opened wide and their mouths dropped open as they felt the cool plaster turn suddenly warm in their hands. They dropped the bags on the table at the same time, looking at each other with surprise and smiles. Kimmy said, "Mine's cooked!"

Foil Squeezing

Materials

aluminum foil

Prepare (Adult)

- Tear off a sheet of aluminum foil.
- Place it on the table or hand it to the child.

Process (Child)

- Explore the foil by squeezing, folding, rolling, tearing, and pressing it.
- Unfold the foil again, if desired.

Variations

- Children can stomp on a foil ball to make an amazing flattened shape. Glue stomped foil shapes to matte board for display.
- Foil can be wrapped around all kinds of objects, bent into sculptured shapes, or fingerpainted upon.

Aluminum foil is remarkably squeezable and makes delightfully tinny sound effects. Children squeeze a sheet of foil until it is a fistful of wrinkles and creases—quite different from the ordinary playclay squeezing experience.

Story

Bethany squeezed and pushed and pressed her sheet of aluminum foil until it was a wrinkled ball. Then she unfolded it and spread it carefully on the table before her, pressing it flat, trying to get all the wrinkles out. "My shiny's gone!" Bethany then wadded her wrinkled foil into a ball, placed it on the floor, and stomped on it with both feet, making it into a very flat foil pancake. Bethany's face lit up like a lightbulb, her grin satisfied and twinkly.

Easiest Bread Dough

The smell of fresh baking bread is a favorite among young and old alike. This easy bread recipe is no exception, offering a cozy fragrance and plenty of good taste. Children do the mixing with help from an adult, children do the creating, and everyone does the eating! These sculptures are best enjoyed warm and soft, fresh from the oven.

Materials

baking sheet
Bread Dough Ingredients
   cooking oil
   dry yeast
   flour
   salt
   sugar
   water
clean towel
cooling rack
floured board
kitchen tools for modeling, such as plastic
   knives, forks, toothpicks, and bamboo
   skewers
measuring cups and spoons
mixing bowl and wooden spoon
oven

Prepare (Adult)

- Make sure everyone washes hands. Assemble all the ingredients.
- With the children's help, mix 1 cup (240 mL) water, 1 teaspoon (7 g) sugar, and 1 tablespoon (20 g) yeast in a bowl until the yeast softens (2–3 minutes).
- Add 1 cup (125 g) flour, and stir vigorously with a wooden spoon. Then beat the mixture until smooth, and add 1 tablespoon (15 mL) oil and 1 teaspoon (7 g) salt. Add another cup (125 g) flour to the dough.
- Pour the thick batter onto a floured board, and add more flour slowly while kneading the dough. (Children love this part.) Keep a coating of flour on the dough to prevent sticking. Knead for about 5 minutes until the dough is smooth, elastic, and satiny. It should bounce back if a finger is poked into it.
- Put the dough in an oiled bowl, and cover it with a clean towel. Place in a warm area, and let the dough rise for about 45 minutes. Then punch it down, and work it into a smooth ball.
- Divide the dough into portions for the children to use.
- Preheat the oven to 400°F (200°C).

Process (Child)

- Mold and shape the dough into sculptures or forms. Use various kitchen tools for modeling, such as plastic knives, forks, toothpicks, and bamboo skewers.
- Place each sculpture on a baking sheet.
- Bake for 15–20 minutes in the lower part of the oven (adult only). Large forms may take longer. Bake until golden and baked through.
- Remove the sculptures from the oven, and cool them on a rack (adult only).
- Eat and enjoy!

Tip

- Children will definitely want to help with the kneading and mixing. To keep their hands from sticking to the dough, place a small bowl of flour on the table for children to dip their hands into while working. Do not be surprised if they like the soft flour as much as kneading the dough.

1 teaspoon sugar

1 teaspoon yeast

Beat vigorously

Story

Ollie had worked with edible dough just one other time, when he helped make sugar cookies. He took it all in stride as he formed his little shapes from the dough and put them on the baking tray. When his once-white bread-dough sculptures came out of the oven all golden and warm, he shouted, "They're cookies!"

Playclay Keeper

Children explore and model shapes with a basic flour and salt playclay (or see page 56 for a recipe for self-hardening playclay); then they press a selection of collage materials into their shapes. Their creations become decorations baked or air-dried into long-lasting sculptures.

Materials
airtight container
Basic Flour-and-Salt Playclay (also called Baker's Clay)
- flour
- measuring cups
- mixing spoon and bowl
- salt
- warm water

collage items (see list)
flat cookie sheet
muffin tin, cups, or other containers, and a baking pan or tray
oven, optional
paper plates
rubber placemat, optional
shallow dish
spatula
tempera paint and paintbrush

Collage Items for Air-drying
- birthday candles
- drinking straws
- feathers
- leaves
- sticks or twigs
- wooden craft sticks

Collage Items for Baking
- aquarium rocks
- pebbles
- shells

Prepare (Adult)
- Make playclay. (Children like to help mix.) Mix 4 cups (500 g) flour, 1 cup (250 g) salt, and 1¾ cups (300 mL) warm water in a bowl. Knead the mixture for 5 to 10 minutes before modeling. This recipe can be doubled or halved successfully.
- Place a rubber placemat in front of each child at the worktable. Put a small portion of playclay onto each placemat. (Children can also work on a bare table.)

  Hint: This clay starts drying when exposed to air. Keep the unused portion fresh by storing it in an airtight container.
- Place loose collage items into the cups of a muffin tin, into paper cups placed on a baking tray, or into any other containers on hand. Spread out other collage items on a baking pan or tray.

Process (Child with adult help)

- Explore and enjoy the playclay.
- Poke, model, roll, and flatten the playclay into shapes.
- Decorate the shapes. Press sticks, twigs, or other materials into the shapes (see list). Notice that some materials are suggested for baking, while others are suggested for air-drying. Choose to air-dry or bake the shapes, depending on the materials that are pressed into them.
- Place the sculptures on a flat cookie sheet to air-dry for several days, or use the following baking directions:

    Bake the shapes at 325°F (170°C) for about an hour (adult only). Use a flat, smooth cookie sheet for baking. The baking time will depend on the thickness of the dough. A good rule of thumb is to allow half an hour of baking time per ¼" (1 mm) thickness of dough. Extra-thin sculptures will bake quickly, so watch them carefully to prevent burning. Allow the shapes to cool.

- After the playclay shapes are dried or baked, pour tempera paint into a shallow dish.
- Paint shapes with tempera paint. Further dry on paper plates.

Tips

- Children love mixing and pouring the water more than any other step of the recipe.
- This dough is not meant to be eaten. However, it will not harm children if it is ingested.
- Children can work on a covered or bare table, individual placemats, trays, or wax paper.

Variations

- *Glaze*—For a shiny surface, glaze the completed shapes before baking by brushing them with a beaten egg white, evaporated milk, or mayonnaise.
- *Handprint*—Make a large flat circle, and ask the child to press her hand in the center. Then bake the playclay, or let it air-dry.
- *Cookie Cutter Shapes*—Roll the dough flat, and cut out shapes with cookie cutters. Poke a hole at the top with the end of a straw before baking. When it is done baking, tie a short or long string through the hole to make an ornament or necklace.

Easy Big Beads

Curious, industrious children love to poke objects through holes, which is why stringing beads is so mentally absorbing for them.

Materials

Homemade Playclay, Self-Hardening
- cornstarch
- flour
- measuring cups
- mixing bowl and spoon
- salt
- warm water

paintbrush or spoon

pie plates

plastic knife

plastic tray or dish

straw, chopstick, or toothpicks

tempera paint

Prepare (Adult)

- Make playclay. (Children will enjoy helping.) Mix ¾ cup (94 g) flour, ½ cup (125 g) salt, and ½ cup (62 g) cornstarch in a bowl.
- Add warm water gradually, mixing it with your hands, until the mixture forms a shape.
- Knead briefly.
- Put the straws, chopsticks, toothpicks, and plastic knives in the middle of the table.
- Plop a ball of dough directly on the table for bead making.

Process (Child)

- Pinch off a piece of playclay, and roll it into a ball. Poke a hole through the ball using a straw, chopstick, or toothpick (adult help and guidance is needed). Roll snakelike shapes, and cut off cylinders using the plastic knife. Adult: Help the children poke holes into the cylinders.
- Place all of the beads on a plastic tray or dish to dry. It will take about one or two days. Turn the beads over occasionally so that they dry evenly.
- When they are dry, paint them or leave them natural. To paint, pour puddles of tempera paint into pie tins. Drop the beads into the paint puddle, and roll them around with a spoon. Or, if preferred, paint them using a brush.
- Place the painted beads on a plastic dish or tray to dry thoroughly.
- For stringing directions, see Stringing Big Beads on the next page.

Stringing Big Beads

String large homemade beads made from self-hardening playclay onto stiff "strings" of thin plastic tubing or plastic lacing. No more frustrated toddlers and twos trying to string beads onto floppy shoelaces or strands of yarn!

Materials

choice of "string"—thin plastic tubing (found in aquarium, hardware, or plumbing stores) or plastic lacing (found in craft stores)

homemade beads (see previous activity, "Easy Big Beads")

other items to string (see list), optional

Items to String

Suggestions for younger children:

    cardboard tubes cut into short lengths

    large, inexpensive wooden beads with big center holes

    thread spools

Suggestions for older children:

    plastic straws cut into 1" (3 cm) lengths stiff, 2" (5 cm)-diameter paper circles with a hole punched out of the center

Prepare (Adult)

- When the homemade beads are dry (see page 56), secure the end of the "string" by putting one bead on the end of the plastic tubing or lacing and tying it securely. This will prevent the rest of the beads from sliding off. The next bead will rest against the first bead.

Process (Child)

- Help the children string the plastic tubing or lacing through the hole in a bead and pull it through. Caution: Always supervise children around beads to make sure that they do not put beads into their mouths.
- String as many beads as desired. If desired, string other objects in addition to the beads, such as plastic straws cut into short lengths or empty thread spools (see list).
- Tie off the last bead to finish.

Tips

- Older children can string beads onto shoelaces or yarn with masking tape wrapped tightly around one end like a large pretend "needle."
- To keep the pieces of straw from springing out of your hands and flying all over, hold them in a paper bag while cutting them.

Variations

- Place the beads in a zipper-closure plastic bag with a small amount of tempera paint. Roll the beads around inside the bag, and watch them become colorfully painted.
- Place several beads and two colors of paint into a paper bag, seal it with tape, and shake the noisy bag to color the beads.
- Sources for ready-made beads: Find a beaded seat cover at a thrift store or garage sale, and cut it apart to get hundreds of large beads. Old costume jewelry can also be a super source. Children can string these along with their own bead creations.
- Make paper beads using sheets of construction paper rolled and taped securely into a 1" (3 cm)-diameter tube. Then cut the tubes into 1"–2" (3–5 cm) lengths.
- Make extra-large paper beads or garlands by wrapping long strips of paper around a broom handle and taping the ends. Then slip off the broom handle and string them on a clothesline.

Story

First Art for Toddlers and Twos *author, MaryAnn, was given the gift of handmade beads created by a toddler who painted each one with watercolor paints before stringing them onto a 3' (1 m) long cord. She has worn them to art workshops for over 15 years, and they are as good as new!*

Silly Dough

*A bouncy exploration for children!
This putty is unusual because it is elastic,
stretchy, moldable, and can be
bounced on the floor like a ball.*

Materials
airtight container
food coloring
liquid starch (Liquid starch comes in half-gallon (2 L) plastic bottles and can be found in the laundry detergent section of the supermarket and often in school supply stores.)
measuring spoons
Silly Dough Recipe (below)
small bowl
spoon
white school glue (not regular white glue)

Prepare (Adult)
- Make the Silly Dough. Mix 4 tablespoons (60 mL) liquid starch, 8 tablespoons (120 mL) white school glue, and ¼ teaspoon (1 mL) food coloring in a small bowl. Let it set for 5 minutes. Note: It's important to use the glue labeled "school glue", and not just any white glue.
- Knead the mixture by hand until the starch is completely absorbed and the color is even. Children enjoy helping to make the dough and especially enjoy kneading.

Caution: Supervise closely to make sure that children do not put the putty into their mouths.
- Store in an airtight container.

Process (Child)
- Stretch and mold the Silly Dough. The more it is kneaded and played with, the better it gets!
- Bounce it against the floor for fun—the rounder the shape, the straighter the bounce. Odd shapes bounce in odd directions.
- If the Silly Dough dries out, dip it into warm water and knead again. Continue exploring.

Variation
- Help the children press the Silly Dough onto an image in the Sunday comics and carefully lift it off. The image will remain on the Silly Dough, just like store-bought Silly Putty.

Story
Barclay bounced his Silly Dough on the kitchen floor as hard as he could for his mommy to catch, but his dough ball went wild and landed in the sink. It then ricocheted to the floor again, where it rolled under the chair. Barclay disintegrated into uncontrollable laughter. Perfect humor for toddlers and twos!

Our task, regarding creativity, is to help children climb their own mountains, as high as possible. No one can do more.

—Loris Malaguzzi, *Founder of the Reggio Emilia Approach*

CHAPTER 3

Making Marks

Making marks may involve scribbling on paper, a sidewalk, a wall, or a table. (If it's the wall, tack up some paper first.) Making marks involves a variety of tools and materials for toddlers and twos to enjoy exploring and mastering—from crayons to chalk to shaving cream to plain water. What wonderful possibilities there are! Crayons are readily available and require no adult assistance, making them the premium choice of all mark-making tools. A material not to be missed is chalk, which has a unique tactile effect. Another great material is shaving cream. Although it might not be considered a drawing tool, the finger that smooshes through it is!

Some toddlers and twos will spend only a minute "drawing," while others will spend a good half hour or more. Expect toddlers and twos to make marks using many styles and methods, and to make them naturally and often. One thing is certain: toddlers and twos need big paper or a big space to make the motions and marks with their large muscles, which is normal and necessary for this age group. (It helps to tape the corners of the paper to the table. When toddlers and twos draw, let them stand and draw instead of drawing while sitting in a chair. This frees their movements and increases creativity.) Making marks delights toddlers and twos and is challenging and absorbing work that involves eye-hand coordination, muscle control, and experimentation with color and design.

Drawing in Sand

Draw again and again through a thin layer of sand covering a dark sheet of paper in a baking pan. Designs can be drawn with a finger, chopstick, or craft stick. And by the way, what is that impressive "scritch scritch scritch" sound?

Materials

dark paper

drawing tools, such as fingers, plastic spoons, wooden craft sticks, chopsticks, and drinking straws

metal baking pan or cookie sheet with low edges

sand (Fine, clean sand from school supply or hardware stores is best, but sifted and cleaned beach or river sand works, too.)

Prepare (Adult)

- Line the bottom of a baking pan or cookie sheet with dark paper.
- Cover the paper with about ½" (2 cm) of sand.
- Shake the pan so that the sand covers the paper evenly.
- Work on the floor or at a low table for this activity.

Process (Child)

- Feel and explore the sand before drawing.
- Draw lines or curves in the sand using fingers, a spoon, or other tools.
- Pat the designs with hands to smooth the sand and start over again.

  Hint: Shake the pan from side to side to remove the drawing and make the sand cover the paper evenly, ready for a new drawing.

Tips

- Because children usually play in an entire sandbox full of sand, they are intrigued by this small amount of sand in a pan and will play with it quite differently.
- The scraping sound of drawing in sand is one of the best parts of sand drawing. Different tools make different sounds.
- Some children do not like having sand on their hands, so keep a soft, old towel handy for brushing off sand.
- Put sand into a cardboard box with short sides instead of a baking pan.

Story

Melissa started out enthusiastically but then was not so sure when the sand got under her nails as she scraped through it to make designs. However, as soon as she realized she could wipe her hands on a damp towel whenever she wanted, she was more comfortable and enjoyed "drawing."

Making Marks

Markers are a basic art supply for children as they progress from scribbling to drawing. Have markers available for independent scribbling and drawing at any time.

Materials

basket or flat tray

markers

masking tape

paper

Prepare (Adult)

- Tape butcher paper to a low table (cover the entire table and over the edges with butcher paper). Be sure to tape the corners.
- Place markers in a basket or flat tray, and put it next to the paper.

Process (Child)

- Scribble freely with the markers.

Tips

- Sometimes it is difficult for a child to pull a tight cap off a marker. An adult can loosen each pen and rest it in the cap.
- If pens start to dry out, dip (or soak) them in water to revive them. The color will get lighter, but you can use this method several times before the marker runs out of color.
- Markers are easy and successful for children to use because only a little pressure is needed to create bright streaks of color.

Variations

- Draw with markers on wet paper to create blurry designs.
- Draw with markers, and then paint over the lines with water to blur the designs.
- Experiment with using markers on different materials, such as aluminum foil, wax paper, coffee filters, and fabric, to see how they behave.

Brightest Chalk Scribbles

Scribble with chalk on a wet sheet of dark construction paper for rich, bright chalk designs that children love. The wet paper is as intriguing for children as the chalk itself!

Materials

colored chalk (wide sidewalk chalk resists breaking and is easy to grip)
dark-colored construction paper
jar lid
paintbrush or wide sponge brush
water

Prepare (Adult)

- Place dark-colored construction paper on the table.
- Fill a jar lid with water, and place a paintbrush or sponge brush next to it.
- Place a few sticks of chalk next to the paper.
- Moisten the paper. Children can paint water all over the paper to soak it, or an adult can hold the paper under a faucet until it is soaked, shake off excess drips, and lay it flat on the table. Children like to help with the water step, whichever way it is done.

Process (Child)

- Children will first be curious about the wet paper and how it sticks to the table.
- After they explore the wet paper, encourage the children to select a piece of chalk and scribble on the wet paper. The chalk marks will be rich and bright.
- Continue dipping the chalk in water and scribbling with it.

Hint: Some children will use their fingers to blur and smear the wet chalk marks.

Tips

- Do not be surprised if children enjoy peeling the wet paper off the table or dipping the chalk in the water. This is all new and interesting work for them.
- If using thin chalk, break it in half so it will not break so easily when children are drawing with it.

Variation

- For less smudgy chalk, wet the paper with buttermilk or liquid starch first. (This will take longer to dry.)

Story

Ashton drew with bright blue chalk on a piece of wet black construction paper until the chalk was nothing more than a little pile of crumbles. He pressed the pile of chalk crumbles into the paper with his finger, smooshing them into streaks as they absorbed the remaining water. Ashton then looked at the other sticks of chalk and pushed his chair back. For Ashton, one color was all he needed to experience chalk on wet paper.

Chalk & Water Drawings

Dip colored chalk into water, and draw. It's so easy! For even more fun, find a puddle of water on the sidewalk, and scribble in it (toddlers and twos love puddles). When chalk is wet, it has a different texture and makes thicker and softer-looking lines. The freedom of scribbling with chalk outdoors anywhere they want is great fun for children.

Materials

berry basket, soup can, or basket
colored chalk (big sidewalk chalk or poster chalk is best)
old scrub brush, optional
sidewalk, driveway, or patio
small bucket of water or a puddle
sturdy wide paintbrush

Prepare (Adult)

- Partially fill a bucket with water, making sure it is light enough for a child to carry easily. Or if possible, find an outdoor puddle on a sidewalk.
- Plunk a big, fat brush into the bucket, or place one next to the puddle.
- Put chalk sticks into a berry basket, soup can, or basket, and head outdoors. (Carry the chalk for the children.)

Process (Child)

- Dip a stick of chalk into the bucket of water or puddle and scribble on the sidewalk.
- Pour a small puddle of water on the sidewalk, and scribble with a stick of chalk in the puddle.
- Put the brush directly into a natural puddle.
- Brush water over chalk lines using a fat paintbrush to blur the lines.
- Scrub off the chalk using an old scrub brush, and then start over again. (Some children love scrubbing. This is a good skill to practice for other potentially messy projects!)

Tips

- Use small buckets of water that the children can carry around independently. Fill each bucket only a few inches deep so children can lift and carry it easily.
- Wrap masking tape around one end of a chalk stick if children do not like the feel of chalk on their fingers.

Story

One day Liza drew with chalk on the cement step in front of her favorite neighbor's house. The neighbor was delighted to come home from work and find Liza's greeting. Eventually, the neighbor told Liza she was disappointed that the drawings had faded away and requested that Liza redo the design for her. As Liza grew older, she continued to draw elaborate pictures and cheerful messages for her neighbor's front step year after year—a friendly tradition that continues still.

Bundle Scribble Box

Draw on a giant cardboard box using large arm movements and a rainbow of colors bundled together with tape.

Materials

large cardboard appliance box
masking tape
washable markers

Prepare (Adult)

- Bundle together a handful of markers (three or more). Make sure all the tips are even by holding the bundle and tapping the tips on the cardboard box. Wrap tape around the bundle.

  Hint: Use tape—rubber bands are not recommended for children.
- Put the box on its side on the floor.

Process (Child)

- Draw all over the box with a bundle of markers. (It's perfectly acceptable to draw with individual markers, too.)
- Scribble on top of the box, down low, while walking around the box, or while jumping up and down.
- Crawl inside, and draw on the bottom of the box, on the sides, or way up high!

Tips

- Visit an appliance store, and ask for an empty refrigerator, dishwasher, washing machine, or TV box. Children love big, big boxes.
- Children love the enclosed space of the box, especially if they can escape easily. Box play is a winner with or without art.

Variations

- Cover the box with wide craft paper or newsprint before children scribble on it. Glue or tape the paper in place (if using glue, let it dry first).
- Bundle together crayons or colored chalk for scribbling, or use them without bundling them together. It's awkward but intriguing to bundle together a variety of drawing tools (e.g., one marker, one crayon, and one chalk) for scribbling.
- Create a play house by drawing lines for windows and doors and cutting the cardboard with a sharp knife (adult only).

Story

Elizabeth was scribbling inside a huge refrigerator box and inadvertently leaned against the bottom, causing the whole box to tip backward. She let out a squeal that was either joy or fright! Soon enough, tipping the box became a favorite game—tipping up and back, over and over again. It was time to put away the markers and crayons and clear the area around the box so the tipping game could continue.

Sandpaper & Stubs

Drawing on new types of surfaces is good for brain development. Discover how different it is to draw on sandpaper instead of drawing paper! Simply color on the rough side of the sandpaper with old crayon stubs, and then iron to melt the drawing.

Materials

crayon stubs
newspaper
old iron (adult only)
paper plate
sandpaper

Prepare (Adult)

- Place a piece of sandpaper, rough side up, on the table.
- Put some old crayon stubs on a paper plate on the table.
- Place an old iron (out of children's reach) on a pad of newspapers. Do not plug it in until later.

Process (Child)

- Color on the rough side of a piece of sandpaper. The crayons will quickly be worn down. This is all there is to it!
- For a further step, an adult can put the crayon-covered sandpaper between two sheets of newspaper and press using a warm iron. This will melt the crayons into the sandpaper. Notice the soft, bright design.

Variations

- Draw on sandpaper using anything that makes marks, such as a cinnamon stick, garden bark, dried-up markers dipped in water, pebbles, and so on. Try all kinds of things to see what happens.
- Draw on sandpaper using crayons. Then an adult can iron this design onto a shirt, pillowcase, napkins, place mat, or tablecloth. Children can even make their own bandanas.

Story

When Winston began to color on the sandpaper, he constantly checked the progression of the quickly diminishing point of his crayon as it went from medium to short with only a few strong strokes. He was equally as fascinated with the crayon's diminishing length as he was with his design.

Scribble It!

Scribbling is a must for toddlers and twos! Increase brain activity by varying the scribbling tools, the materials on which to scribble, and the places to use the materials. Not to sound too much like Dr. Seuss, but "in a box, on a fence, on the floor, on a door..." is only the beginning! Mix and match tools, materials, and areas to scribble for hundreds of possibilities.

Materials

Mix and match the following tools, materials, and areas to work. Feel free to add your own ideas to this list!

Prepare (Adult)

- Choose a tool, a material, and a place to scribble. It's best to start with only one of each.
- There are hundreds of possible scribbling activities you can achieve by mixing and matching one item from each column on the next page. Try your own ideas! For example, children can scribble using:
  - a marker on a coffee filter clipped to an easel
  - a crayon on a rock that is under a chair
  - a sponge dipped in water, paint, or food coloring on a paper plate hung on a wall

Process (Child)

- Scribble freely using the selected tool on the selected material in the selected place.
- Supply more than one material, and help the children change materials as needed.

Tip

- Start with only one tool, one material, and one area. Later, try different tools with one material. Make changes when children seem ready.

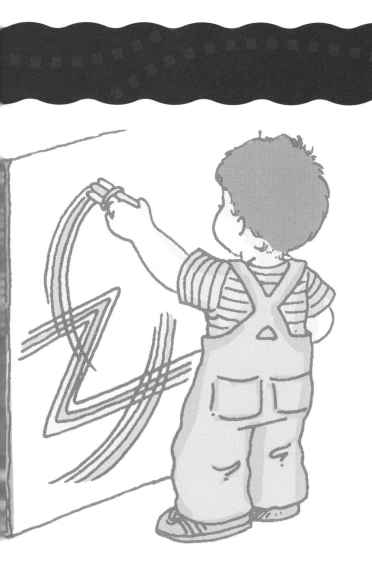

Scribbling Tools

bingo marker

chalk

charcoal

cotton swab

dipped in food

coloring

craft stick

crayon

craypas (oil pastels)

finger, hand, or foot

food coloring

highlighter pen

marker

olive or baby oil

paints and brush

pastels

pen, any kind

sponge

squeeze bottle

stick

warm or melted crayon

Scribbling Materials

calendar, old

cardboard, any

cardboard box

cereal box

coffee filter

coloring book page

comics

greeting cards, old

junk mail

magazine page

matte board

napkin

newspaper

origami paper

paper, any kind including

bond, construction, and

drawing

paper plate

paper towel

rock

sidewalk

warming tray

window

wood scrap

wrapping paper or tissue

Scribbling Areas

in a box

in a garden

in a park

in a swimming pool

in a tent

on a book or magazine

on a chair

on a door

on a fence

on a lap

on a sidewalk

on a tray

on a tree

on a wall

on a window

on an easel

on someone's back

on the floor

on the grass

on the underside of a table

under a chair

under other paper

under a bed

Dibbidy-Dab Draw

Explore a fun-filled, active, draw-with-paint technique using sponge-tipped bingo bottles. Fill them with bright, thin paint, and then dab, draw, or make entertaining splats and bubbles.

Materials

2–3 bingo bottles (small, plastic squeeze bottles with sponge tips, available from school supply or office supply stores)

2–3 bright colors of thin tempera paints, or liquid watercolors

light-colored paper, any color or texture

tape

Prepare (Adult)

- Fill bingo bottles (or other small bottles with sponge tips) with bright-colored, thin paint.

  Hint: Bingo bottles are used for stamping bingo numbers or for a variety of office uses. They are commonly available for children's art from craft and school supply stores.

- Place light-colored paper on the table. If desired, tape the corners of the paper to the table to prevent it from slipping.

- Put two or three paint-filled bingo bottles beside the paper with the lids removed, sponge tips ready to go.

Process (Child)

- Press the sponge tips on the paper. Push, pound, smear, draw, and squeeze the tips on the paper. Each action makes a different mark, design, or pattern.

  Hint: Squeezing the bottle with the sponge tip on the paper will form tiny bubbles of paint—a favorite for toddlers and twos. Tapping or dabbing the sponge tips will make little splatters and sometimes bubbles.

- Try different colors of paint and experiment with different types of papers.

Tips

- Pounding and slamming bingo bottles into paper is a natural reaction for active children exploring this art experience for the first time. Be understanding, but encourage them to use more gentle motions.

- To refill bingo bottles, pop out the sponge tip, and slowly pour paint into the bottle. A small kitchen funnel will help control the paint flow.

Variation

- *Roll-On Draw and Paint*: Fill clean roll-on deodorant bottles with paint. To do this, remove the bottle's plastic collar and ball as a unit. While pressing a thumb hard against the collar, pry a screwdriver underneath to pop off the collar and ball. Then clean out the bottle, fill it with tempera paint, and snap the collar-and-ball unit back on. Hold the bottle upside down, and roll the ball end across the paper to draw with paint.

Story

Cilla discovered how to make little bubbly sunburst designs by tapping the sponge tip of the marker with minimum downward force on her paper. Each tap produced a sunburst.

The Need to Squeeze

Squeezing thick paint dough from plastic bottles onto matte board is easy and satisfies the children's need to squeeze. Watching the paint dough ooze out and the colors pool together is a joy for toddlers and twos.

Materials

base paper, such as matte board, cardboard, or paperboard (cut-up cereal boxes)

electric beaters, if needed

flour

large bowl and wooden spoon

measuring cups and spoons

plastic squeeze bottles, such as squeeze bottles from school supply catalogs, plastic condiment bottles, or empty glue, ketchup, mustard, or shampoo bottles

salt

small bowls

sturdy paper

tempera paint

water

Prepare (Adult)

- With the children, mix 1 cup (240 mL) water, 1 cup (250 g) salt, and 1 cup (125 g) flour in a large bowl until completely smooth. (If you use empty glue bottles for squeezing, use electric beaters to whip the mixture for a few minutes to make it totally smooth, or the flour clumps may clog the small hole.)

- Add liquid tempera paint, 1 teaspoon (5 mL) at a time, until a desired color is reached. To make several colors, separate the mixture into smaller bowls, and add a different color to each one. This recipe can be easily doubled, tripled, or more to make additional colors.

- Make a funnel by curling a piece of sturdy paper into a funnel shape. Slip the funnel into the mouth of the squeeze bottle, and pour the mixture into the bottle. Or, just spoon the mixture slowly into the bottles.

- Tighten the lids, and place the bottles on the worktable.

- Place base paper, such as matte board, in front of each child.

I CUP SALT

I CUP WATER

I CUP FLOUR

Process (Child)

- Squeeze the bottles, forcing the puffy paint onto the matte board or other base paper. Children will first want to squeeze simply for the joy of squeezing, and later will be more likely to actually draw.
- Squeeze several colors on top of each other to see how they refuse to blend and instead form interesting related pooling shapes.
- When finished, let the dough drawing dry. The drawing will have a puffy look, drying hard and bright with a little glitter from the salt.

Tips

- When children get their hands on a bottle of glue, they love to squeeze it all out. This activity is the perfect legitimate art project for their need to squeeze! You may need to snip a larger hole in the tip of the glue bottle so the thick paint comes out easily.
- Paint dough disappears quickly, so consider making a double batch.
- A generic condiment bottle is a child-favorite squeeze bottle. The hole is big, and the plastic is easy to squeeze. It is also easy to fill because the bottle opening is large. You can snip the tip off the bottle to form a larger hole.
- Children get the giggles over the funny *ploop-ploop* noise the bottles make as the paint dough begins to run out.

Story

Jarone squeezed and squeezed until his bottle was empty. On his cardboard square was a pile of colored dough in stringy noodle shapes. He smiled and said, "I like to squeeze!"

Draw & Paint Black Magic

Lines appear like magic! Draw with black crayon on black construction paper, paint over it with water, and watch the crayon lines magically jump into view.

Materials

black construction paper
black or dark purple crayon
shallow dish
variety of paintbrushes
water

Prepare (Adult)

- Fill a shallow dish with an inch or less of water.
- Place the dish on the table with black construction paper, black crayons, and a variety of paintbrushes.

Process (Child)

- Scribble with black crayon on black construction paper.
- Dip a paintbrush into the dish of water.
- Then, paint over the black crayon scribbles and over the black paper. See how the crayon lines suddenly appear more vibrant.

Tip

- Brushes come in many widths and degrees of softness. Let the children experiment with a variety to see which is most successful.

Variation

- Try scribbling on red paper with red crayon, white paper with white crayon, green paper with green crayon, and so on. Then paint over the scribbles with water.

Story

Rika put her black paper on the floor to work, as she often does for other art projects. She has more leverage when she can kneel over her paper and apply her coloring muscles to the task. Rika has never made a crayon resist before but likes the challenge of coloring "hard." When she paints over the crayon marks with water, she is surprised and very pleased with how her design is easier to see. Rika adds more water to see what else might happen. When the project does not change significantly with additional water, Rika gets a second sheet of paper and begins scribbling again using her strong coloring muscles.

First Crayon Resist

Paint with watercolors over crayon drawings, and watch how the wax in the crayons resists the watery paint! This is an "oooo-ahhh" basic-but-essential art project.

Materials

crayons

paper

paper plate

shallow dish of water

tempera paint

wide paintbrushes

Prepare (Adult)

- Place a variety of crayons on a paper plate on the table.
- Put a sheet of paper in front of each child's chair or standing spot by the table.
- Pour tempera paint into a shallow dish of water to thin it. Set aside the dish of thinned paint and paintbrushes until the children are finished coloring.

Process (Child)

- Scribble hard on the paper with crayons. Light, scratchy scribbling is acceptable and appropriate for children, but it will not produce as bright a result as hard scribbling using big muscles. Experimenting with and repeating this project often will help children see the difference.
- When finished, dip a wide paintbrush into the thinned paint.
- Paint over the crayon scribbles, and watch how the paint resists the wax of the crayon. (Keep in mind that young children's crayon resists can be very drippy!)

Tip

- Cover the table with a plastic tablecloth and layers of newspaper. Then, if a child tips over the water, the newspaper can absorb it quickly.

Variations

- Draw with white crayons on white paper or with other same-color combinations of paper and crayons (e.g., red crayon on red paper, yellow on yellow, and so on). Children will be astonished when the crayon markings suddenly appear bright and dramatic after painting over them.
- Use liquid watercolors to produce very bright results.

Story

Liam came to the conclusion that coloring with big muscles was what crayon resists were really all about. He wanted to prove that his muscles were all that and more! He was coloring with jumbo crayons on large paper, so he had plenty of room to test—and improve—his skill. Liam stuck with the coloring until he was sweaty—even his T-shirt was damp and warm. What pride he had in his "big muscle" work!

First Rubbings

Crayon rubbings are a basic art experience for older children, and now young children can enjoy them too with this easy approach.

Materials

masking tape
objects to rub (see list)
oil pastels or chalk
variety of drawing tools, such as old markers and peeled jumbo crayons or crayon stubs (darker colors, such as purple, blue, and magenta, work best)
white paper

Objects to Rub

flat items wrapped in paper (such as flat cheese grater, metal grill, window-screen scrap, and wire cake-cooling rack)
heavy paper
keys
large buttons
large coins
leaves
scraps of cardboard
wrinkled foil
yarn

Prepare (Adult)

- Place a variety of objects to use for rubbing on a low table.
  Hint: It might be a good idea to secure smaller items to the table with a loop of masking tape. This will help prevent them from slipping and tearing the paper.
- Place a large sheet of paper on top of the rubbing items, and tape it to the table.
- Wrap individual flat items in paper of their own, such as a cheese grater, cooling rack, or grill rack. (See Variations for suggestions.)

Process (Child)

- Scribble on the paper using oil pastels or other rubbing tools. Notice how the raised items underneath create patterns on the paper.
- Experiment using different objects under the paper and different drawing tools.

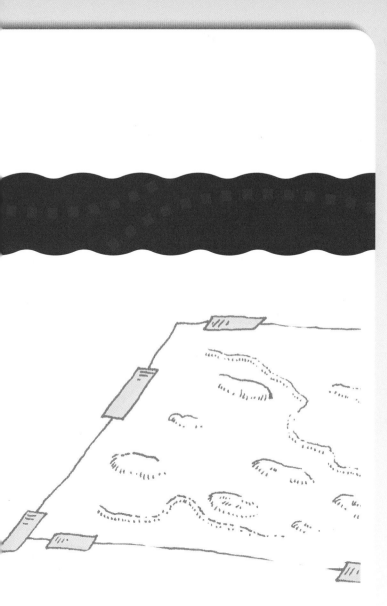

Tips

- To peel crayon stubs easily, soak them overnight in water. Then, slip off the paper from the crayons.
- Children often have a difficult time holding peeled crayons on their sides. Scribble Cookies (see recipe to the right), oil pastels, and markers are easier for them to use. Use old markers because this activity wears markers out.
- Keep in mind that children's first experiences with rubbings will not have "adult-experience-level" results. Be pleased with the children's scribbly-scratches, as they are appropriate and necessary for children to progress to more advanced work.

Variations

- Try rubbing cutouts of letters, squiggles of yarn, or geometric shapes cut from cardboard.
- Make crayon rubbings at the easel. Tape a few shapes under the easel paper, and then rub crayons over them.

Scribble Cookies Recipe

Save stubs of crayons. Peel the paper from the crayons, and break them into small pieces. Choose to sort them by color into an old muffin tin or mix colors to make rainbow discs. Place the muffin tin into a warm oven that has been turned off. Watch carefully as the crayons melt and soften, floating in liquid wax. Remove them when they are partially melted (but not liquid pools), and let them cool. To easily remove Scribble Cookies, freeze them while they are still in the muffin tin, and they will pop right out. Let them thaw briefly before using. Break them in half to give the artists a flat side and a round side for rubbings or coloring.

Story

Lily likes peeling the paper from crayon stubs. She has excellent pincher control and can peel tiny bits of paper from a crayon stub. She shakes her fingers to loosen the paper scrap, which floats to the floor next to her chair. But the floor can be easily swept later, and helping peel crayons is hard work with a happy reward—art!

Art stimulates the imagination and makes the child think more inventively…

—Barbara Herberholz and Lee Hanson, *Early Childhood Art*

CHAPTER 4

Sticky Business

The action of sticking things to other things is the most valuable part of a child's exploration of pasting, tearing, and assembling. It is not the finished product itself that will delight toddlers and twos; it is the process of exploring, experimenting, and discovering exactly what "sticking" means in all its wonderful forms. Toddlers and twos will sort and dig through collage materials, fascinated and intrigued by the choices. They will explore sticking things together using tape, paste, glue, and other materials that help things hold together. When children begin experimenting with these materials, they often just feel the paste, glue, or tape with their fingers, exploring the sensory qualities of these materials. Later, they cover paper scraps with other scraps and items, heaping and layering, using a ton of glue or tape and a lot of "explore-gusto."

While they are enjoying these experiences, they are refining the small muscle control in their hands and fingers. During these beginning stages, providing limited materials in smaller containers controls things a bit. As toddlers and twos become more experienced, increase their choices and materials. It is important to note that scissors are not necessary in the beginning stages of art. Do not expect children to master the cutting of paper with scissors until they are well over three years old, but do expect them to have fun as they discover how! Step-by-step suggestions for helping children learn to cut with scissors are given at the end of this chapter.

List of Collage Materials

Supervise use of all materials. Be sure that the materials are safe for the children who will be using them.

A
acorns
aluminum foil

B
balsa wood
bamboo
bark
basket reeds
beads, large
belts
bias tape
bingo markers
blotter paper
bottle caps (large)
bottles
boxes
braiding
broken toys
buckles
burlap scraps
buttons (large)

C
cancelled stamps
candles
candy wrappers
cans
cardboard scraps
carpet samples
cellophane scraps
cellophane tape
chains

chalk
checkers
clothespins
cloth scraps
coffee filters
coins
combs
confetti
construction paper
scraps
contact paper
cord
corks
cornhusks
costume jewelry
cotton
cotton balls
craft sticks
crepe paper scraps

D
dominoes
drapery samples
dried flowers
dried grass
driftwood

E
Easter grass
egg cartons
eggs, plastic Easter
elastic
emery boards

embroidery thread
embroidery hoops
erasers
evergreens

F
fabric scraps
feathers
felt scraps
filters
flocking
florist's foil, foam
tape
flowers
flowers, artificial
flowers, dried
flowers, plastic
foam
fur samples

G
gauze
gift wrap
glitter
gold costume jewelry
gold jewelry parts
gold thread
greeting cards
gummed labels
gummed paper
reinforcements
gummed paper

H
hair netting
hair rollers
hardware items
hardware scraps
hat trimmings

I
ice cream sticks
inner tube scraps

J
jars
jewelry pieces
jewelry wire
junk of all kinds
jute

K
key rings
key tabs
keys

L
labels
lace
laminated items
leather scraps
leaves
lids
linoleum scraps

M
mailing tubes
masonite
meat trays, paper
meat trays, plastic
meat trays, foam
mosquito netting
moss, dried

N
newspaper

O
oilcloth scraps
orange sticks
origami paper
ornaments

P
paper baking cups
paper cups
paper dots
paper fasteners
paper products, all
    kinds
paper tubes
pinecones
Ping-Pong balls
pipe cleaners
plastic bottles
plastic foam
plastic scraps
plastic, all kinds

Q
Q-tips

R
raffia
recording tape
ribbon
rickrack
rope pieces
rubber tubing

S
sandpaper
screening, plastic
    or wire
seals
seals, gummed
seam binding
seashells
sewing tape
shoelaces
silk scraps
sponges
spools
spray can lids
stamps, all kinds
sticks
stick-dots
straws, broom
straws, drinking
straws, stirring
string

T
tape, general variety
tape, cellophane
tape, library
tape, masking
tape, plastic
tape, sewing
tape, transparent
thread
tiles
Tinker Toy parts
tissue paper
tongue depressors
toothbrushes
torn paper scraps
twigs
twine

U
ukulele strings

V
velvet scraps

W
wallpaper
wax candles
weeds
wood scraps
wood shavings
wooden beads
wooden dowels
wooden wheels

wool
wrapping papers

X-Y-Z
yarn
zipper-closure bags
zippers

Press & Stick Collage

Children pinch and then sprinkle and pat collage items onto sticky contact paper for an easy, no-glue, first "stick-it" experience. Children love picking up tiny objects, which is the focus of this activity.

Cut a large rectangle of clear contact paper...

Peel off the backing, stopping at the fold...

Materials

bowls
clear contact paper (adhesive-backed vinyl)
piece of cardboard
scissors
selection of tiny collage items, such as birdseed, unshelled sunflower seeds, and sand
spoons
tape

Prepare (Adult)

- Cut out a large rectangle of contact paper from the roll.
- To make a convenient "handle" for holding the rectangle, press a sharp 3" (8 cm) fold into one short side of the rectangle.
- Peel off the backing, stopping at the fold. Cut off the peeled backing. This 3" (8 cm) "handle" area with the backing in place makes it easier to hold onto the contact paper and move it around without it sticking to hands.
- Tape the corners of the contact paper, sticky side up, to a piece of cardboard (about the same size as the piece of contact paper) for easy handling and moving.
- Place each of the collage items into separate bowls, and put the bowls within easy reach of the children.

Process (Child)

- Feel and explore the collage items before making a collage.
- When ready, pinch and sprinkle tiny collage items onto the sticky area of the contact paper using fingers. Or use spoons to drop items onto the sticky paper.
- Completely cover the sticky side of the contact paper with collage items so it is no longer sticky anywhere.
- Tape collage in the window to catch the sunlight (adult).

Tips

- Create an ongoing collage-materials collection in a shoebox or plastic tub with a snap-on lid. Collect random items to add to and pull out for each collage project. Include cotton balls, pieces of fabric, feathers, bits of foil and waxed paper, confetti, dots from hole punches, cut-up junk mail, tissue paper, wrapping paper, ribbons, and any other bits and pieces as they come along. (See the collage list on pages 80–81.)
- Margarine cups make great yarn holders. Poke a small hole in the lid, place a ball of yarn in the cup, and pull the loose end through the hole in the lid. Snap on the lid, and the yarn will unroll without tangling.
- Keep a small dustpan and broom handy for children to sweep up their own spills. They love to sweep!

- To pick up small items, moisten a fingertip using a wet sponge, and press the item onto the sticky paper.

Variations

- *First Mural*: Tape a large sheet of peeled contact paper to the wall, sticky side out, at child height. Stick any items on the contact paper. Choose items that can be removed and stuck on again, such as jar lids, and other items that will stick permanently, such as magazine pictures.
- *Tacky Walk*: Tape a huge roll of contact paper (sticky side up) to the floor, remove shoes, and walk across the sticky walkway (with adult help).
- *Press-It Mesh*: For children who prefer nonsticky fingers, cut off a length of cupboard liner (the kind that looks like loosely woven rubber mesh), and tack it to the wall. Press lightweight items onto it, which should stick for some time. Start with yarn and paper scraps. Easy on, easy off!

Tape corners of rectangle sticky-side up to cardboard...

Story

Claire carefully picks up a tiny hole-punched paper dot and then firmly presses it to a piece of contact paper. She pats it with her palm and stands back to observe her work. Satisfied, she reaches into the container of paper dots and grabs a small handful, which she presses to the sticky paper. Many stick, and some fall to the floor, which is fine with Claire.

Touch & Pour Explore

Touch, pour, and explore! Children can plunge their hands into tubs filled with collage materials that allow them to play as they explore how to handle the materials. Allow ample playing and exploring time before moving on to the collage experience.

Materials

collage materials (see list)
cups, spoons, and clean, empty tuna cans
dishpans or tubs
glue
old sheet or blanket
paintbrush
pieces of cardboard or matte board
shallow containers

Collage Materials

aquarium rocks, clean
beads
birdseed
buttons
confetti
cornmeal
cornstarch
cotton balls
fabric scraps
foam packing pieces
nuts in shells
pebbles
sand
seeds
sunflower seeds, unshelled
yarn scraps

Note: Supervise the use of these materials.

Prepare (Adult)

- Spread an old sheet or blanket on the floor to mark the exploring space and to catch spilled collage materials. (If desired, use a small towel or mat and smaller containers.)
- Pour 2 to 4 cups of each collage material (see list) into separate dish tubs.
- Pour small amounts of glue into shallow containers. Put one or more paintbrushes into each container.
- Set aside pieces of cardboard or matte board to use as backgrounds for the collage. Bring these out after the children have sufficiently explored the collage materials.

Process (Child)

- Use hands to feel and explore the collage materials, letting them flow and pour through fingers and hands.
- Pour and explore the materials using cups, spoons, and cans (which are wonderfully noisy). Use duct tape to cover any rough edges of the cans, though rough edges are uncommon.
- After the children have explored the materials, bring out the glue, brushes, and cardboard so the children can make a collage.
- Paint glue onto the cardboard.
- Pour or sprinkle collage materials onto the sticky glue, and shake off extra materials into the tub. Allow the collage to dry overnight.

Tips

- Children love to sift their fingers through seeds or other materials. It feels great! Give them lots of time to explore. Supervise materials closely so children do not put items in their mouths.
- Children respond very well to keeping materials within a space that is defined by a blanket or sheet. They can help clean up by lifting the sheet and pouring the collage materials back into a tub.

Variation

- *Seaside Collage*: Create a collage on a piece of cardboard using brightly colored aquarium rocks. These have a unique texture and feel and are wonderful for sifting and pouring possibilities. They are also delightfully noisy! Add other seaside materials to the collage, such as shells, dry seaweed, or driftwood.

Story

David's play group had two dishpans filled with collage materials for the children to explore: one with large bottle caps and one with seashells. The children were fascinated with pouring and handling the materials that were so different from traditional sand or water experiences. David particularly enjoyed adding toy kitchen utensils. He was busy and focused for a long period of time.

Collage Fun— Four Favorites

Collecting and saving materials to use for collage is fun for everyone. Choose materials that are appealing and that have variety in their textures and feel. For example, puffy soft cotton balls, silky feathers, pokey golf tees, and fragrant items from nature are but a few that toddlers and twos will especially enjoy.

Stick-On Cotton Balls

Make the softest collage ever by gluing cotton balls onto colored paper!

Materials

colored paper
cotton balls
cotton swabs
glue
shallow containers
tray

Prepare (Adult)

- Pour glue into shallow containers. Rest a cotton swab on the side of each dish of glue, with one end in the glue.
- Place a tray of cotton balls within easy reach of the children.

Process (Child)

- Drip or dab glue on the paper with a cotton swab. Then, stick cotton balls onto the dots of glue.
- Dab and dip cotton balls into the dish of glue, and press them onto the paper. (Do not be surprised to see children tickling their own faces, necks, eyelids, and arms with the soft balls before gluing.)
- Tip: Children love to explore and play with the cotton balls before using them in a collage.

Stick-On Golf Tees

Not every collage needs paste, glue, or tape— hammering is another way to make things hold firm. Successful hammering is exciting and easy for toddlers and twos, and good practice for hammering real nails into wood later on.

Materials

chunks of foam
golf tees
tape
toy hammers or mallets
yarn, ribbons, string, or paper scraps, optional

Prepare (Adult)

- Tape a block of foam to a low table or floor so it will not slip or flip.
- Arrange materials, hammers, and golf tees on the work area.

Process (Child)

- Press a golf tee gently into the foam block base until it stands up by itself.
- Hammer the tee into the foam using a toy hammer. Continue with more tees.
- For variety, drape yarn, ribbon, or string from golf tee to golf tee, or pound tees through paper scraps to add to this colorful collage. Tees can be removed and used again. Children can also hammer the tees into sand or dirt.

Hint: Children love to feel and sift through the golf tees before using them.

Stick-On Nature

Children can make a collage that is also a nature collection.

Materials

cardboard
glue in shallow containers such as jar lids
natural materials, such as sticks, leaves, acorns, and small rocks
newsprint
paintbrushes or spoons
paper lunch bag
scrap of wood or heavy paper plate, optional

Prepare (Adult)

- Go on a nature walk outside with the children to collect sticks, leaves, acorns, and small rocks. Put the items into a paper lunch bag.
- Back inside, spread the contents of the lunch bag on a piece of newsprint.

Process (Child)

- Brush or spoon glue onto a piece of cardboard.
- Press one of the collected items into the glue, continuing to add more to complete the collage. Allow the collage to dry for at least one hour.
- For variety, glue nature items to a scrap of wood or a heavy paper plate.

Stick-On Feathers

Children can glue bright, light fluffy craft feathers onto a paper plate or a shape cut from a manila folder.

Materials

colorful craft feathers
paper bowl, optional
paper plates or manila folders
scissors, optional
tray or shallow box

Prepare (Adult)

- Open a craft bag of feathers.
- Place the feathers on a tray or in a shallow box.

Process (Child)

- Brush glue on a paper plate or cut-out shape.
- Stick feathers into the glue in any design. Allow it to dry.
- For more feather fun, glue feathers to a paper bowl to make a silly hat.
  Hint: Watch for allergic reactions to feathers, such as sneezing or watery eyes, though craft feathers are usually not a problem.

Easy Paste & Paper

Fabulously sticky and thick, homemade paste is a wonderful tactile experience for toddlers and twos. And because children in this age group love to tear paper, combining paper and paste is a sure winner for involved, contented exploration!

Materials

base for artwork, such as cardboard, matte board, file folder, or paperboard (cereal boxes)

box or tray

flour

measuring cups and spoons

paste applicators, such as cotton swabs, craft sticks, plastic glue sticks, or plastic knives, optional

peppermint extract for fresh scent, optional

saucepan and wooden spoon

selection of paper (see list)

small, heavy dish

stove top or hot plate (adult only)

sugar

tape

water

Papers for Pasting

construction paper

magazine pages

newspaper

old calendar

old comics

pages from old coloring books

Sunday comics

tissue paper

used telephone book

white paper

Prepare (Adult)

- Make Homemade Paste (children love to help): Mix together 4 tablespoons (80 g) sugar and 2/3 cup (80 g) flour in a small saucepan. Slowly add 2 cups (480 mL) water, and stir vigorously to break up the lumps. Cook over low heat, and stir constantly. When the mixture is smooth and clear, remove it from the heat. Stir in ½ teaspoon (2 mL) peppermint extract, if desired. After the mixture has cooled, scoop it into a heavy dish to prevent the container from sliding around when the children put their fingers into it.

- Tape a base for the artwork, such as cardboard, to a low table.

- Place a selection of paper scraps (see list) into a box or tray, and put it on the table, along with the heavy dish of paste and paste spreaders (optional).

Process (Child)

- Tear paper into strips and small pieces. (Tearing is a big part of this activity for children.)
- Dip fingers into the paste, and explore the sticky feeling.
- Smear the paste onto the cardboard, somewhat like fingerpainting, or dip a cotton swab or craft stick into the paste, and stir or spread.
- Stick pieces of torn paper on hands or on the sticky cardboard.

Tips

- Approach pasting as a fun, free-form activity. Give children a few objects such as craft sticks to dip into the paste, but do not expect the children to really understand how to spread paste and stick something on top the first time. Pasting is a fairly complex process that children will master when they are older.
- Toddlers and twos love the feeling of their hands working in opposition by tearing large sheets of paper. They also love the loud sounds of tearing paper, especially if several people are tearing paper at once.
- Some children love the sticky feel of paste on their hands, while others may not. Encourage finicky children to use spreading tools such as wooden craft sticks or plastic sticks. Most young children enjoy pasting, and like to use paste like fingerpaint. They are intrigued by the sticky feel on their hands and like to pinch their sticky fingers open and closed.
- Children like to stick tiny paper scraps on their fingertips and pull them off again.

Stir vigorously...
Cook over low heat...

Scoop onto a heavy dish when cool...

Paper Paste Explore

Glue strips and scraps of different kinds of paper to create a unique collage. This is a great exploration activity. Collect a variety of paper scraps for children to feel and compare during this collage experience. Repeat this enjoyable experience often.

Materials

choice of interesting papers (see list)
construction paper
foam grocery trays, shoebox lids, or paper plates
glue
paintbrush
scissors
shallow dish

Paper to Save

bakery bag, white
butcher paper
construction paper
foil or metallic paper
grocery bag, brown
hole punches, punch dots
magazine pages
Mylar sheets
newspaper
old photographs
paper towels
Sunday comics
tissue paper
wallpaper
wax paper
wrapping paper
writing paper

Prepare (Adult)

- Prepare a variety of papers (see list) for children to explore. Cut each of the papers into small strips or scraps that are easy to manipulate.
- Put a different type of paper scrap into each tray or lid.
- Pour glue into a shallow dish, and put a paintbrush next to it.
- Give each child a piece of construction paper for the base.

Process (Child)

- Brush or drizzle glue onto the construction paper.
- Choose a variety of paper pieces, and press them into the glue on the construction paper to create a collage. Some children will create a sparse design, and others will heap them on!

Tips

- Papers that are crinkled slightly before or after cutting are easier for children to pick up than flat papers.
- Collage explorations will vary widely based on the materials that are collected or selected. Repeat this experience often with new materials, or bring back favorite materials anytime. Children enjoy repeating projects over and over, which also improves their skills.
- Egg carton cups work great as glue or paste cups, and cotton swabs are great for spreading or dipping glue.

Variations

- Make a collage using a variety of stickers, labels, sticky dots, sticky stars, or scraps of fabric with glue.
- *No-Glue Mural*: Secure a large piece of contact paper to a wall or large cardboard box with masking tape, sticky side facing out. Arrange the cups of paper scraps on the floor in front of the contact paper. Press the pieces of paper onto the contact paper.
- *Make a Collage Book*: Staple a few pieces of paper together. Then glue paper scraps, photos, or magazine pictures to the pages.

Story

Cara glued one small foil square onto a big piece of blue paper, looked at it, and said, "That's all!" Although urged to add more, Cara was satisfied that her creation was complete and just the way she wanted it to be.

Easy Suncatcher

Tissue paper pressed on sticky clear contact paper makes a beautiful first suncatcher to hang in a sunny window.

Clear contact paper

12"

6"

Fold contact paper in half...

Pull protective backing off to the fold...

Materials

clear contact paper

hole punch

scissors

scraps of art tissue or colored wrapping tissue

small piece of string or yarn

Prepare (Adult)

- Cut or tear art tissue scraps or colored wrapping tissue into pieces about 1"–2" (3–6 cm) wide.
- Cut out a 6" x 12" (15 cm x 30 cm) piece of contact paper.
- Fold the contact paper in half lengthwise to make a 6" x 6" (15 cm x 15 cm) square.
- Pull the protective backing halfway off (to the fold), and place it on the table, sticky side up. You may wish to tape the contact paper to the table.

Process (Child)

- Press tissue scraps on the sticky exposed side of the contact paper until satisfied with the design.
- Peel off the remaining protective backing of the contact paper, and fold it over the decorated side. (This step requires adult help.) Press firmly. An adult can cut off the sticky edges, or cut the square into a more circular shape.
- Punch a hole (adult only) in the top of the design, and tie a string through it for a window hanging.

- Choose a favorite window, and hang the suncatcher.

Tip

- Contact paper can be hard to handle for both children and adults, so do not worry too much about wrinkles, lumps, or bubbles that form when the children press the sticky sides together.

Variations

- Stick reflective or see-through art materials, such as clear scraps of cellophane paper or metallic confetti, on the contact paper.
- *Paper Plate*: Cut out the center of a paper plate, and use the remaining edge as a frame for a suncatcher.
- *Glue Art*: Squeeze white glue onto wax paper, and press colored paper, confetti, or other colorful items into the glue. Let the glue dry for several days until it is transparent and hard; then peel it from the wax paper, and hang it in the window.

Simply Stickers

Peeling and pressing stickers on paper is a brand-new skill for most toddlers and twos. They will enjoy exploring the sticky characteristics and discovering the permanence or "peelability" of their endeavors.

Materials

any background paper, such as construction paper, cardboard, or a paper plate
markers and crayons
selection of stickers (see list)
wide, shallow box

Sticker Possibilities

address mailing labels
Band-Aids in a variety of shapes
computer diskette sticker labels, cut into quarters
file-folder sticker labels, cut in half
foil stars
holiday stickers
round, colored dot stickers
sheets of novelty stickers

Prepare (Adult)

- Gather and save stickers in a wide, shallow box. Place the box on the worktable.
- Select any kind of paper or cardboard on hand and place it on the table.

Process (Child)

- Dig through the stickers, looking at and feeling all the different kinds.
- Choose one or several stickers. Peel the stickers from the backings, and press them onto paper. (Save the borders from around the stickers; they can be used for sticking, too!)
- Scribble or draw over the stickers on the paper with markers and crayons. Watch how the markings react as they move over the paper and cross over the stickers.

Tip

- Gently peel some stickers from the backings, and press them to the edge of the table with one edge exposed so children can easily pull them off as needed.

Story

Warren peeled white mailing labels from their backing, one at a time, sticking them onto a piece of white matte board. Some were wrinkled or bubbled, but Warren was content. Then he took a red crayon and began scribbling over the white labels and the white background. As he did so, the crayon bumped over the label edges, creating bright red and lighter red effects and patterns, which he found wonderfully satisfying. He also enjoyed the bumpy noise his red crayon made as it moved back and forth over the labels.

Sticky Tape Collage

Handling tape is tricky sticky business, but it is great fun and highly motivating for children! Making a simple collage is an easy way for toddlers and twos to explore handling and experimenting with the variety of tapes available.

Materials

baking pan, optional
paper
scissors
various types of tape (see list)

Variety of Tape

cellophane tape
clear packing tape
colored masking tape (narrow and wide, available in craft or school supply stores)
double-sided tape
duct tape
electrical tape (in different colors, found in hardware stores)
masking tape, common beige variety
pink hairdo tape
pre-cut tape pieces (office store)
surgical tape
transparent tape

Prepare (Adult)

- Prepare a variety of tapes. Cut or tear off several 4" (10 cm) strips of each kind of tape, and stick them to the edge of a low table (or the edge of a baking pan). The tape ends should extend off the edge so that the children can pull off the pieces easily and without help.
- Place paper in front of each child's work area.

Process (Child)

- Pull off pieces of tape, and stick them on the paper in any design, pressing down the edges and overlapping them (if desired).

Tips

- Do not be surprised—children often stick tape to themselves or other things! Tape reminds children of Band-Aids, so the urge to put tape on their hands and legs can be irresistible.
- Tear off small pieces of tape, and stick them around the top edge of an empty plastic dish tub so the tape pieces are easy to peel and use. Or, fill the tub with sand, rocks, or a beanbag to weigh it down to prevent it from slipping. Put the cover back on, and put small pieces of tape around the edges.
- Invest in a heavy, office-style tabletop tape dispenser or purchase packages of precut pieces of tape. Even though children might not master cutting off small pieces of tape from the dispenser until they are older, this is the first type of dispenser they will be able to use successfully. To make it easier, attach the dispenser to the table with masking tape so it will not slip when the child tries to use it.
- Remember that some types of tape remove paint from surfaces or walls.

Building Blocks Sculpture

Dip wood scraps into glue, and build a sculpture—one, two, three, build it up! Four, five—how high can we go?

Materials

base for the sculpture, such as a square of cardboard, matte board, or flat piece of wood

glue (Tacky Glue™ or Sobo™ works best)

glue brush

shallow dish

tempera paints and brushes, optional

wood scraps with smooth edges (see list)

Wood Scrap Possibilities

balsa wood scraps

framing scraps from a frame shop

lumber scraps

wood scraps from a construction site

wood scraps from a woodshop class

wooden beads

wooden spools

wooden toy blocks from a thrift store

Prepare (Adult)

- Place the sculpture base, such as a cardboard square, near the table's edge.
- Pour glue into a shallow dish, and place it next to the base, along with a glue brush.
- Arrange a variety of wood scraps so children can reach them easily.

Process (Child)

- Dab a puddle of glue on the sculpture base.
- Dip scraps of wood into the glue, and stack them like building blocks. Or, brush glue on the scraps instead of dipping them into the puddle.
- Let the sculpture dry overnight.
- If desired, paint the sculpture with tempera paints the next day.

Tips

- Use smooth wood pieces to avoid splinters.
- Instead of using glue, an adult can use a cool glue gun or help the children tape unruly wood scraps together with masking tape to hold them while the glue dries.

Story

Lily loves creating and exploring with art materials. Nathan, Ellen, and Paul are busy dipping blocks of wood into glue and stacking them on squares of matte board (two, three, four, and even five blocks high!). Lily dips a wood scrap into glue and presses it to her matte board. She takes another scrap and presses it next to the first. Lily continues to dip and press scraps of wood, covering her matte board in one layer of blocks, close together like a puzzle, a completely unique approach in the midst of active tower building.

Foil Wrapping

Children wrap silvery aluminum foil around cardboard shapes, pressing and pinching it to fit, discovering foil's unique gripping characteristics.

Materials

cardboard or wooden shapes, or small boxes
heavy-duty aluminum foil

Prepare (Adult)

- Tear a stack of aluminum foil from a roll and further tear into squares, and fan them out on the worktable.
- Arrange cardboard shapes or small boxes on the worktable.

Process (Child)

- Wrap foil around cardboard shapes, pressing and pinching it to fit.
- Cover and wrap the shape until satisfied.

Tip

- Children like to stack their finished foil pieces into tall towers, enjoying how they tumble down again.

Variations

- Provide brightly colored tape to join shapes together.
- Stick shapes to a background with loops of masking tape to make a 3-D collage.

Easy Weave

Children discover that tape and glue are not the only ways to hold things together. A three-dimensional way is to wrap, tie, and weave materials together.

Materials
box or tray

masking tape

scissors

six-pack holder (plastic rings)

two wooden blocks

weaving materials (see list)

yarn and kitchen chair, optional

Weaving Materials
blanket, old

construction tape

crepe paper

fabric

felt

newspaper

paper

plastic bags cut into strips

raffia

surveyor's tape

torn T-shirt

wide ribbons

Prepare (Adult)
- Tape two blocks to a table, about a foot (30 cm) apart (the same width as the six-pack ring).
- Tape the plastic six-pack ring between the two blocks to make a stable weaving space (see illustration). If desired, you can also use yarn to secure the six-pack ring between the back of a chair and the front of the seat.
- Cut pieces of weaving materials (see list) into strips, and place them in a box or on a tray.
- Put the strips of weaving materials next to the plastic six-pack ring.

Process (Child)
- Weave a strip of material in and out of the holes of the six-pack rings.
- Choose strips of material, and push them in and out of the holes—tying, wrapping, knotting, and weaving in and out until satisfied with the weaving.

(Continued on the next page)

Tips

- Children's first experiences with weaving will be very random and tangled, often knotted and lumpy. This is expected, appropriate, and wonderful!
- Strips between 1' to 2' (30 cm to 60 cm) are easiest for children to manage. Experiment with other lengths to see what works best for individual abilities.

Variations

- Weave strips of material through construction fencing that is attached to a wall or a fence.
- Weave materials through a laundry basket.

Story

Marcus pulled a strip of plastic bag from the box. At first he could not quite figure out how to make it hold to the plastic rings. He pressed it to the edge of a plastic ring, and it fell to the floor. Then he pushed it through one hole where it hung precariously for a moment and then floated down to the floor. Marcus was not deterred. He picked up the strip and wrapped it around and around and around through one hole of the plastic ring. It held. Then he added strips of plastic until the ring was completely puffy with plastic.

Early Scissors Experiences for Toddlers and Twos: The Three Stages

Toddlers and twos are intrigued by scissors: how they open and close, how they magically cut paper, and how adults like to keep them out of their reach! The safest first-scissors experience for toddlers and twos is to let them cut thin playclay rolls (known to children as "worms" or "snakes"!). A good second experience is to help them cut small strips of yarn held taut by an adult. Finally, the more advanced third experience is to let them cut strips of construction paper independently. An important note: Do not expect children to master cutting paper with scissors until they are well over three years old, but do expect them to have fun as they learn how!

Stage 1—Worm Factory

Opening and closing scissors is the most difficult part of cutting for beginning artists. Cutting rolls of playclay into pieces is an easy, motivating, and satisfying early cutting experience.

Materials
blunt-tipped, all-plastic scissors
Playclay (see recipe, page 49)

Prepare (Adult)
- Put playclay and scissors on a low table.
- Ask the children to sit on small chairs at the low table.

Process (Child)
- Poke the playclay with the scissors, separating the ball into pieces.
- Roll playclay pieces into long, thin "worm" shapes.
- Cut or snip the ends of the "worms" into pieces using scissors.
  Hint: Children may wish to explore the clay and the scissors this first time. Cutting the rolls into worms may not happen the first time, or even the second time. But once the children master holding the scissors and cutting the playclay, they will spend hours cutting clay worms into many, many pieces.

Tips
- Young children enjoy playing with safe scissors that have no sharp edges. They will practice opening and closing scissors, and they will hold them in unique ways as they learn how to use them. Encourage exploration as the children poke and prod the playclay and cut it using the scissors like a knife.
- All scissors work should be done while sitting down. This will help teach children to sit while using scissors.
- Children should sit in chairs that allow their feet to touch the floor during cutting activities. This gives them more stability.
- Most children will try to use both hands to open and close the scissors at first. Any techniques they explore are good.
- Supervise all scissors use by young children.

Variation
- Use scissors to cut Silly Dough (see page 59), Playdough (see page 44), Baker's Clay (see page 54), and other modeling recipes.

Early Scissors Experiences for Toddlers and Twos (Stage 2)

Stage 2—Yarn Factory

Once children can handle scissors and open and close them with one or both hands, they are ready to cut yarn. Pull the yarn taut for children so they can cut in the middle of the strand.

Materials
blunt-tipped, plastic preschool scissors
  (choose blunt-nosed scissors with a
  sharper cutting edge, such as Fiskars™)
yarn or string

Prepare (Adult)
- Precut several long strands of yarn or string, and place them on the table.
- Place the preschool scissors on the table.
- Sit on a short chair facing the child (who is also on a short chair), or sit on the floor facing each other.
- Pull a piece of yarn taut between both of your hands.

Process (Child)
- Cut the yarn using preschool scissors.
  Hint: Taut yarn is easier to cut than loose strands of yarn.

Tips
- Leave yarn scraps on the table for children to explore, or pick up a large scrap so the child can cut it again. As children get older, they enjoy cutting these scraps into tinier and tinier pieces.
- Preschool scissors are usually made of plastic with a sharper metal cutting edge imbedded on the edges. These scissors can cut yarn and paper easily. It's best to give children quality scissors that will yield successful cutting than to give them overly blunt scissors that do not cut well. However, always supervise scissors use. Remember that even preschool scissors can nick skin.
- Remember, scissors can also cut hair! Children have been known to cut their own hair or the hair of their friends, who are usually quite willing to have their hair cut.

Variations
- Tape about 10 lengths of yarn across the top of a baking pan for children to cut independently.
- Tie loops of yarn around a paper towel tube for children to cut apart.
- Save scraps of yarn or other threads for other art projects.
- Use embroidery thread or dental floss instead of yarn.

Early Scissors Experiences for Toddlers and Twos (Stage 3)

Stage 3—Paper Factory

Many older children will be ready to cut paper strips after they have mastered cutting playclay and yarn. Then they can experience the freedom and wonder of cutting with scissors!

Materials

plastic preschool scissors with sharper cutting edge (quality brand) or quality scissors for smaller hands, such as Fiskars™

shoebox or empty baby wipes plastic box

stiff paper, in a variety of colors and textures

Prepare (Adult)

- Cut stiff paper into strips about 2" x 6" (5 cm x 15 cm). Use a variety of colors and textures, if possible.
- Place the paper strips in the box.
- Place the box of strips and scissors on a low table.

Process (Child)

- Sit at the worktable in a small chair. (Be sure the children sit in chairs while working with scissors.)
- Cut strips of paper with scissors.
  Hint: Initially, the adult can hold the paper strips taut as the child cuts down the middle. Then, the child can try cutting independently.
- Cut the strips into smaller strips, square pieces, or even wavy pieces.

Tip

- Supervise children carefully around scissors. They enjoy showing their cutting mastery on hair, clothing, towels, and toilet paper when they get a chance.

Variations

- Tape large loops of paper strips to the edge of a cardboard box or table for children to cut independently.
- Tape a very long strip of paper to the table, making wavy loops and taping each segment along the way. Snip each segment. Save all scraps for other art projects.

"... **each stage of children's drawing development is very precious, and will never come again.**"

—Mia Johnson, *Understanding and Encouraging Your Child's Art*

Johnson, Mia. 1993. *Understanding and encouraging your child's art*. Los Angeles: Lowell House.

CHAPTER 5

Great Impressions

Printing is a simple method with a simple concept: press an object in color, and see the design on paper. Perfect for young children! Toddlers and twos need little introduction or encouragement with printing. "Press it here, and press it there" is about all they need to know! Toddlers and twos especially enjoy using their own hands and feet to make prints. Other favorite printing experiences are using tinted bubbles that pop designs on paper, or driving toy cars through color and then making tracks on paper.

The secret to keeping toddlers and twos happy while making prints is to tape their papers to the worktable to keep the papers from tearing or wiggling. Sometimes children like the noise of printing as much as the colors and design! *Slap, click, pound, bumpity-bang, clunk,* and *screech!* As with all art exploration for children, the process of printing will capture their enthusiasm more than any finished printed work.

List of Printing Possibilities

Supervise use of all materials. Be sure that the materials are safe for the children who will be using them.

A

animals, toy plastic

acorns

B

back scrubbers, variety

balls, any variety

bath puffs, mesh

berry baskets

Bingo daubers

blocks

body parts (hands, feet, toes, fingers, elbows, knees)

boots

bottle caps

brayers

brooms, child size or full size

brushes, all kinds

bubble wrap

bumpy things: glued to cardboard, paper towel tubes, or gloves

buttons

C

cans, dipped in paint to make circles

cardboard, pieces

cardboard, with string glued on it

carpet and upholstery samples

cars, toy

casters

checkers

clothesline

clothespins

combs

containers with shaker tops

cookie cutters

corks

corncobs, dried

craft sticks

crayons, paint

crayons, wax

crepe paper

D

dandelions

deodorant bottles

dishwashing brushes

dominoes

E

egg cartons

eyedroppers

F

fabrics, different textures

feather dusters

feet

fingers

flowers

fly swatters

foam, pieces of

foil balls

forks

funnels

G

gadgets

gelatin molds

gloves

golf balls

H

hair rollers

hands

I

ice cubes

J

jar lids

junk, variety

K

keys

kitchen utensils

knobs

Koosh balls

L

leaves

lids: from jars, containers, bottles

M

markers, dried out

mashers

meat tenderizer mallets

molds

mops

muffin tins

N

newspaper, crumpled

nylon stockings

P

paint rollers

panty hose, foot filled with sand

paper cups

paper towel tubes

pinecones

pine needles

plastic lids

plastic wrap, crumpled

plungers

poker chips

Popsicle sticks

potato mashers

Q

Q-tips, cotton swabs

R

rolling pin, with fabric or yarn wrapped around

rolling pins, general

rubber stamps, old

S

scouring pads

seashells

shoes

soap trays with soft bumps

soap trays with suction cups

socks filled with sand

spatulas

sponges, cut up or full size

sponges, in shapes

spools, old thread

spoons

sticks

strawberry baskets, plastic mesh

straws

string or yarn

T

toothbrushes (run through dishwasher)

toes

toy cars

toys, any with wheels

toys, broken parts of

V

vinyl tiles

W

wallpaper-smoothing brush

weather stripping, self-adhesive foam

wheeled toys

wood scraps

wooden carpentry rosettes and trim accents

Y

yarn, general varieties

yarn, glued around paper towel tube

yarn, wrapped around rolling pin, cardboard, or wood scrap

Busy Printing

Hunt for print-making objects! Tools, kitchen utensils, toys, and ordinary objects will produce designs, shapes, textures, and delightful surprises.

Materials

foam grocery trays

large paper, variety

masking tape

paint, different colors

printing tools (see list on this page and additional suggestions on pages 104–105)

trays

wet paper towels

Prepare (Adult)

- Select a few printing tools (see list), and put them on trays.
- Spread a large sheet of paper on the table. Tape down.
- Make a printing pad by folding a few squares of paper towels together and holding them under a faucet to moisten. Place them in a foam tray, and pour a puddle of paint on the towels. Do this for each color of paint in each tray.
- Place trays of paint near the printing tools. Place a loop of masking tape on the underside of each tray to secure it.

Printing Tools

cookie cutters

corks

corncobs

cotton swabs

egg whisks

erasers, big

feather dusters

flyswatters

foil balls

foot & toe pads

hairbrushes

pine needles

pine tree branches

plastic cups

playdough balls

potato mashers

rags

rolling pins

shoe soles

socks filled with sand

sponges

string

thread spools

toy cars

toys

Process (Child)

- Dip one of the printing tools into the paint (in the foam tray), and then press it on paper to make prints. The following are some ideas and techniques:
  - Dip a flyswatter, egg whisk, or pine branch in paint, and swat or hit the paper.
  - Roll a rolling pin in paint, and then roll it over the paper to make a zigzag pattern.
  - Dip thread spools, cookie cutters, or a potato masher in paint, and press on the paper.
  - Pour a puddle of paint in the center of the paper, and press a cork, hairbrush, or comb into the paint and then on the paper.
  - Stick foot pads on a rolling pin, and roll it in paint and then on the paper.

Tip

- Do not be surprised if children scrub and rub the printing tools on the paper to see what the paint will do, eventually even tearing through the paper. They are exploring how the tools and paint behave; experimenting is to be expected and final products are not the main goal.

Variations

- Cut dried sponge sheets into any shapes, and use them for printing. For fun, rehydrate them in a bowl of water before making prints.
- *Favorite T-Shirt*: Print on a T-shirt with print tools or hands dipped in fabric paint from a hobby store. (Put a layer of newspaper inside the shirt first so the paint will not soak through.) Allow the shirt to dry completely overnight, and then put it in the dryer by itself for four minutes to set the color, or follow the fabric paint instructions. Expect—and enjoy—"child style" printing designs!

  Hint: Fabric paint is permanent, so protect clothes, nearby surfaces, and children.

Fingertip Prints

For an easy first printing experience, children can dip their fingertips into food coloring and dab circles and patterns of color on a white paper towel.

Materials

food coloring
shallow, flat, heavy dishes
tablespoon
water
white paper towel squares

Prepare (Adult)

- Spread white paper towels on top of a newsprint-covered table.
- Mix about 1 tablespoon (15 mL) water and 4 drops food coloring in each dish to make "dyes," and place them near the paper towels. Heavy, flat dishes work best, as they do not tip over easily.

Process (Child)

- Dip fingertips into the dyes, and then touch the paper towel to make dabs of color, working randomly or making patterns. Color absorbs quickly into the paper towels.
- The design will air-dry quickly.

Tips

- Children often wipe their fingers on their clothing, so have them wear old art clothes for this project. Have damp sponges on the table for wiping hands and fingers.
- Food coloring can stain hands but will wash off in a few days with regular washing.

Variations

- Explore using a cotton swab instead of fingers for dipping and dying.
- Surprise! Look at the newsprint under the paper towel to see "secondary" art.
- Press fingertips or thumbs onto an inked stamp pad and then onto paper.
- Do fingertip prints on baby wipes for a tie-dye look.

Story

Skyler dipped a finger into red food coloring and gingerly pressed it on a paper towel, watching as color was absorbed and created a fat, red dot. Then he dipped two fingers into the blue color and made fat, blue dots and a few streaks. Next he dipped all five fingers into the yellow color and pressed those on the paper towel. Skyler picked up his paper towel design, held it up to the light, turned it over, and looked at both sides, noticing that the pattern had soaked through. "See?" he said in descriptive one-year-old speech, "See my? See my!"

Sit-Down Paint Dancing

Put on some bright and lively music! Children can make giggly paint-dance prints on large paper using their bare feet, rain boots, or old shoes, when they sit on chairs, dip their feet into paint, and then, without standing, dance their feet on the paper

Materials

bare feet, rain boots, or old shoes
butcher or craft paper, around 2' x 3'
    (½ m x 1 m) or any convenient size
child-height chairs
dishpan or tub of soapy water
dishpan or tub, and paint
old towels
tape

Prepare (Adult)

- Tape a sheet of paper beneath a child-height chair.
- Pour about 1 cup (240 mL) of paint into a dishpan or tub, and place it next to the chair.
- Place old towels and a tub of soapy water next to the chair.

Process (Child)

- Ask the child to sit on the chair, and place the tub of paint on the paper so the child can dip one foot or both feet into the paint. Then remove the tub.
- Turn on some lively music.
- While seated, press and dance feet on the paper until the paint no longer makes prints. If desired, redip feet, or add new paper.
- When the child is finished, first wipe her feet with an old, dry towel. Then help her put her feet in the soapy tub of water, and wipe her feet dry. (Additional cleaning may be needed.)

Tips

- Newspaper printers often sell roll ends of unprinted newspaper for a low price. The roll is usually 12' (4 m) wide, and the printer will saw it in half to make two 6' (2 m) rolls. The rolls of newsprint are great for big projects or footprint art.
- Some children do not want to get their feet or hands messy. Provide optional choices for them, such as covering their feet with old socks or boots.

Variation

- Walking on a long sheet of paper and making footprints is great fun. Either paint the bottoms of children's feet with a paintbrush (oh, that tickles!), or children can dip their feet into tubs of paint and then walk with adult assistance down a long sheet of paper. Place a tub of soapy water and old towels at the end of the paper for easy cleanup. (Walking backward is fun, too!)

Zooming Wheels

There's no such thing as a reluctant artist when a child discovers rolling the wheels of toy cars, trucks, and tractors in paint and then making colorful tracks by zooming them across paper. Guaranteed delightful—complete with sound effects!

Materials

baking pan, cookie sheet, or tray

big paper

small toy cars and trucks with different wheel sizes and textures (Any wheeled toys are great—small airplanes, cars, wagons. Keep them as painting tools and only rinse, or soak them overnight in soapy water to remove the paint. No need to return them to the toy shelf.)

tempera paint

Prepare (Adult)

- Place the big paper near the edge of the table so children can reach it easily.
- Place vehicles at the top edge of the paper, and the tray to the side of the paper.
- Spread a thin layer of paint in the tray.

Process (Child)

- Roll the wheels of the car (or other wheeled toy) in the paint. Then drive it over the paper, watching for all the different tracks that are made.
- Make tracks with different wheeled toys and colors of paint.

Tips

- Toys can be rinsed and dried and placed back in the toy box, but relegating old toys to art use reduces clean-up requirements significantly!
- Cover the entire table with paper or do this activity outside on the driveway or playground.

Variations

- For multiple colors of paint, put out four smaller trays, each with a different color of paint. Put one car in each tray. Cars will end up in all of the trays, colors mixing often and in many ways.
- Tape a marker onto a toy car, allowing the marker to just touch the paper. Push cars around the paper, making colored lines.

Story

Quinn broke into a wide grin, clapped his hands, and said, "Quinn likes trucks!" He rolled the toy truck in paint and then rolled it on paper without needing any introduction. Roll it in the paint; roll it on the paper! What Quinn added to his painting experience were sounds like you might hear at a construction site busy with trucks and bulldozers: "Vunn, vunn, vunn; vvvrrroooom, vvvrroooom; voooom, voooom;" and "brrrrapraprap," to name but a few.

Tilt & Roll Dotted Track

Place a paint-covered golf ball in a shallow paper-lined box. Gently tilt or shake the box, and the ball will leave a dotted track of paint wherever it rolls. Golf balls are noisy and exciting!

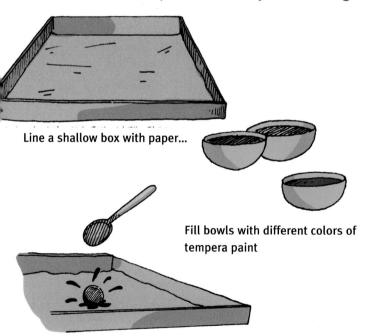

Line a shallow box with paper...

Fill bowls with different colors of tempera paint

Materials
golf balls
paper
shallow cardboard box with 3" (8 cm)-high
    sides, clean kitty litter tray, or baking pan
small, heavy bowls
spoons
tempera paint

Prepare (Adult)
- Line the bottom of the shallow box with paper.
- Fill bowls with different colors of tempera paint, and place them on the table.
- Drop golf balls in each bowl of paint, with children's help.
- Spoon a wet, paint-covered ball from the bowl, and plunk it into the box, with children's help.
- Start with one ball in the box. Two or more can be added later.

Process (Child)
- Tilt and tip the box to roll the balls around and see the paint tracks they make on the paper.
- Add balls from different paint colors, and roll them at the same time.
- When done, soak balls in a tub of soapy water, and wash by hand. Dry with old towels. Washing the golf balls also cleans hands!

Tips
- Children love to roll the balls around in the paint with a spoon. They may use their hands to transfer the wet balls to the box. Let them experiment.
- Toddlers and twos are exuberant, and golf balls sometimes escape. Consider it part of the fun.

Variations
- Using any round objects, consider doing this project in a children's small wading pool or washtub instead of a box. The fun of a wading pool is that children can work together to tilt the pool to make the objects roll through paint. The following are some suggested objects:
  - dog ball
  - Koosh ball
  - Nerf ball
  - playground ball
  - super bouncy ball
  - tennis ball
  - whiffle ball
  - yarn ball
- Line the bottom of the box with aluminum foil or wax paper instead of paper.
- Repeat this activity in any containers lined with paper, such as a coffee can with lid snapped on, a potato chip or tennis ball can with lid, a round cake pan, or a dish tub.

The Blob!

Printing paint blobs is a classic children's art experience. Brush and drizzle paint on the open paper, then fold and press. Open to discover a symmetrical, one-of-a-kind, mixed-color design (and more designs within that design!).

Materials
construction paper
old rolling pin, optional
shallow dishes
spoons
tempera paint

Prepare (Adult)
- Prefold sheets of construction paper, unfold, and stack them opened flat on the worktable.
- Put paint in shallow dishes, and place a spoon in each dish of paint.

Process (Child)
- Spoon blobs of paint colors around the center of the paper, on or near the fold.
- Refold the paper, and gently rub the top of the paper with open, flat hands to spread the paint inside. Children also can use a rolling pin to roll over the paper, pressing the paint into designs.
- Help unfold the paper to see the amazing symmetrical blob design.
- Make as many paint blobs as the child's interest dictates.

Tips
- To help control the amount of paint dripped on the paper, use a wooden craft stick instead of a spoon.
- Young children tend to blob the paint anywhere on the paper.
- Expect paint to squeeze out from between the paper onto the table.

Variations
- *Flower Blob*: Cut out blobs, and glue them on a mural of a garden, each blob being a blossom or flower.
- *Monster Blob*: Cut out blobs, and glue them on white paper. Draw legs, eyes, or other features to make the blobs into monsters, creatures, or cute imaginary pets.

Story
Susan dipped her spoon in blue paint and dripped it over her paper, making big blue spots and wiggly designs. Susan scooped up some yellow paint in her spoon and poured it on the paper, dragging the spoon through the blue spots and wiggles. Next, she folded the paper over with a little help, and she pressed and patted the paper with one hand. When she unfolded the paper, she was astonished that her designs were gone, and in their place, a huge blue, yellow, and GREEN splotch had bloomed. She put her finger out, touched the wet design, and then looked up as if to ask, "Did I do that?"

Easy Bubble Prints

Blowing bubbles is wonderful fun for toddlers and twos. With colored bubble soap, they can see what shapes the bubbles make as they pop on white paper—a great outdoor project.

Materials
food coloring
large sheet of white paper
masking tape
small bottle of bubble soap with bubble
    blowing wand
teaspoon

Prepare (Adult)
- Tape the large sheet of paper to a table, wall, fence, or garage door at child height.
- Mix ½ to 1 teaspoon (2–5 mL) food coloring into each bottle of bubble soap. Make one for each child.
- Hand each child an opened bubble bottle. Help them find the wand inside.

Process (Child)
- Stand very near the white paper, and blow bubbles, trying to aim them at the paper. **Hint:** Wands will get very slippery with soap.
- *Whee! Pop!* When colored bubbles hit the paper, they pop and make circular patterns of color.
- Try another sheet of paper, or turn over the first sheet, and cover the other side with popped designs.

Tips
- Dip and hold the wand for the children to blow bubbles if they have trouble managing by themselves. Child-friendly, spill-proof bottles of bubble soap are available at school supply, toy, and many discount stores.
- Make a strong bubble soap with dishwashing liquid and a little water, but be aware that it can sting a little if bubbles pop in children's faces. See recipe on the next page.

Variations
- Indoor version: Blow bubbles onto a single sheet of wet paper set up at a worktable.
- Yogurt cups with lids make great bubble blowers. Poke two holes in the lid. Insert a straw through one hole and leave the other open. Fill cup with bubble solution and snap on the lid. Child blows through the straw, and bubbles pour out the other hole and down the sides of the cup. **Hint:** Prick a small hole near the top of the straw. This will allow children to blow out but prevents them from sucking in.

Big Buncha Bubbles

A large-group recipe, better than commercial bubbles

Materials

1 part soap—liquid dish soap, such as Joy™ or Dawn™ (not Ivory)

10 parts water

1 tablespoon (15 mL) food coloring

1 teaspoon (5 mL) glycerin (if desired, substitute corn syrup)

Mix well, and let sit overnight.
Pour into bubble bottles, or use from cups, jars, or bowls.

Easy Homemade Bubbles

Miss Angie's suggestion for an easy bubble recipe

Materials

food coloring, any color

pipe cleaners (chenille stems)

¼ cup (60 mL) strong dishwashing detergent

1 teaspoon (5 mL) sugar

½ cup (120 mL) water

Prepare bubble mixture, and divide into small paper cups. Mix a different color of food coloring into each cup. To make bubble wands, bend and twist the ends of pipe cleaners (chenille stems) to form circles. Use white paper to catch colored bubbles.

Story

Miss Angie likes to unroll a white roll of paper across the table so a group of children can make bubble prints together. They stand above or slightly to the side of the paper and gently blow colored bubbles. As soon as a bubble pops, a colored bubble design appears on the paper. What fun!

Impressive Burlap

Printing through—instead of with—burlap is a new printing concept for children and adults alike. It makes an impressive textured design.

Materials

foam grocery tray or pie pan
masking tape
old rolling pin or brayer (craft roller), optional
paper
squares of loose-weave burlap fabric
stiff paintbrush
tempera paints

Prepare (Adult)

- Find scraps of burlap about the same size as a sheet of drawing paper, or cut pieces to size.
- Spread tempera paint in a grocery tray or pie pan. Place loops of masking tape on the base of the paint pan, and stick it to the table to prevent spills. Put one or several puddles of paint in the tray.
- Place a stiff paintbrush next to the paint tray.
- Put a piece of paper on the table with a stack of extra paper nearby. Have an old rolling pin or brayer handy for an optional rolling and pressing activity.
- Place the burlap scrap on top of the sheet of paper. Tape down to hold, if needed.

Process (Child)

- Dab paint directly on the burlap with the stiff paintbrush, letting the paint go through the weave of the fabric to the paper beneath.
- When children are satisfied with the painting, peel the burlap off of the paper and see the textured design that remains. (Children may need adult help with this step.)
- Repeat. This time, when finished painting, roll the burlap with an old rolling pin or brayer to smooth and press the paint into the fabric. Now remove the burlap, and see the textured print beneath.

Tip

- Taping the burlap to the paper and to the table prevents it from wriggling or smearing, and helps children achieve a clear print.

Story

Caity dabbed red paint on the square of red burlap with the white paper underneath it. She was trying to cover all the little white squares that were showing through the material. When she was done, an adult helped her peel the burlap from the paper. Caity was sincerely surprised, delighted, and quite satisfied to see the white paper with red dots that was produced by her painting efforts.

Bubble Wrap Print

Bubble wrap is fun to explore—feeling the puffy bubble pouches and noisily popping them. After exploring, bubble wrap becomes an intriguing printing material with captivating artistic results.

Materials

bubble wrap (any size bubbles), approximately 9 ”x 12” (25 cm x 30 cm) or larger. (Big bubbles make big dots, and little bubbles make little dots.)

large sheets of paper

masking tape

newspaper

paintbrush

shallow baking pan

tempera paints

wet sponge

Prepare (Adult)

- Protect the table with newspaper, if needed. Then place a sheet of bubble wrap on the table, taping down the corners to hold.
- Place a shallow baking pan next to the bubble wrap. Put several puddles of different colors of paint in the pan. Place a paintbrush next to the pan. If needed, place loops of masking tape on the base of the pan to keep it from sliding around the table.
- Have a stack of extra paper handy for multiple prints. Be sure the paper is larger than the sheet of bubble wrap.

Process (Child)

- Paint directly on the bubble wrap with as many colors as desired. The more colors, the merrier!
- When the bubble wrap is covered with colors, press a sheet of paper onto the bubble wrap, and lift off a multicolored print. (Adult help will be needed.)
- Remove the print to a drying area, and repeat with fresh paper. If the bubble wrap becomes murky with color, simply wipe it off with a wet sponge, and begin again.

Tips

- Allow children to explore feeling and popping the bubble wrap before expecting them to paint on it. Who can resist popping those clear, smooth bubble pouches? Let children pop and play first, and the painting activity will go much more smoothly.
- Toddlers and twos are often more captivated by mixing the paints in the baking pan than by painting on the bubble wrap.

Variations

- Explore lifting prints from other textured materials. The following are some suggestions:
  - aluminum foil, crumpled and opened
  - burlap scrap
  - grass
  - gravel path
  - muffin tin
  - plywood scrap
  - welcome mat
  - wire screen
- Explore lifting prints from items glued to cardboard. The following are some suggestions:
  - buttons
  - Bingo markers or checkers
  - bottle caps
  - masking tape
  - Band-Aids
  - yarn
  - string
  - leather strips

Place 2 or 3 colors of paint in a pan...

Story

Jeannette pushed and pushed the bubble wrap pouches with her fingers, her thumbs, and her hands. Nothing she did seemed to make them pop like Charley's, whose bubble wrap was almost completely flat and popped out! Finally, she put her piece of bubble wrap on the floor and jumped on it with both feet. It worked!

Big Stamp & Roll

Children who have explored and experimented with everyday printing items are ready for the large-muscle challenge and excitement of a big wooden block stamp and a big rolling pin print-roller!

Big Wood Block Stamper

Materials
extra-large paper (butcher paper or craft paper)
large tray or baking pan (bigger than the wood block)
old computer mouse pad
paper towels, moistened
scissors
12' x 12' (30 cm x 30 cm) scrap of flat wood
tempera paints
white glue or glue gun, optional (adult only)

Prepare (Adult)
- With children's help, cut any shapes, designs, or letters from an old mouse pad (or any thick material such as cardboard), and glue to one side of a big flat scrap of wood. Let dry overnight or until firmly set and dry.
- Place the moist paper towels in a tray to make a printing pad, and pour some tempera paint on the towels. It's fun to put several colors of paint on one pad. Making more than one tray of paint is fine, too, but save this for a second or third stamp-and-print experience. One tray of paint is good for a child's first experience.

- Place the tray, block, and a very large piece of paper on newspaper on the floor. Taping the paper down will help in case the wood block sticks to the paper and lifts it off the floor.

Process (Child)
- Press the big wood block, design side down into the pad of paint. Then press it on the paper to make a print. Press with both hands and maybe even a knee. It is possible to make more than one print before more paint is needed.
- Press the block in paint again, and continue making prints until satisfied.

Big Rolling Printer

Materials
glue

large tray or baking pan

old wooden rolling pin, used for art activities

paper

paper towels, moistened

tempera paints

yarn

Prepare (Adult)
- With children's help, wind yarn around the old wooden rolling pin. If necessary, use glue to hold yarn permanently.
- Follow paint and paper preparation steps for the Big Wood Block Stamper.

Process (Child)
- Roll the rolling pin through the paint on the tray.
- Then roll it on the big paper, watching how the yarn leaves wiggly tracks and prints.
- A long roll of paper makes this experience extra fun.

Variation
- Consider sticking other materials on the wood block or the rolling pin that will make interesting prints:
  - Band-Aids
  - bunion and corn pads, unused
  - cardboard shapes
  - contact paper shapes
  - felt or other fabric scraps
  - shapes cut from tire inner tubes
  - insoles for shoes, unused and cut into shapes or pieces
  - thick tape

Story
Mackenzie peeled and pressed unused new bunion and corn pads to the rolling pin used for art activities. She covered the wooden cylinder and then rolled it on the bare table, listening to it "bumpity bump" over the surface and getting the idea of how to roll a rolling pin. Next she rolled it in paint, and then began rolling it across the big paper. She rolled it across the paper until all the paint was faded. The funny thing was that she had been kneeling and had "walked" on her knees right through her paint design. Wearing art clothes took the worry out of learning how to manage the rolling pin.

"Imagination is more important than knowledge."

—Albert Einstein

Viereck, G. S. 1929. What life means to Einstein. *The Saturday Evening Post*, October 26, 1929.

Indexes

Index by Icons

Supervise Closely and Use Caution

Outdoor Area Suggested

Good Group Activity

Index